"This series is a tremendous resourc[e] ... [i]n understanding of how the gospel is ... [an]d pastors and scholars doing gospel bu[ilding] ... [theo]logical feast preparing God's people to ~~apply~~ ~~the entire Bible~~ to all of life with heart and mind wholly committed to Christ's priorities."

> **BRYAN CHAPELL,** President Emeritus, Covenant Theological Seminary; Senior Pastor, Grace Presbyterian Church, Peoria, Illinois

"Mark Twain may have smiled when he wrote to a friend, 'I didn't have time to write you a short letter, so I wrote you a long letter.' But the truth of Twain's remark remains serious and universal, because well-reasoned, compact writing requires extra time and extra hard work. And this is what we have in the Crossway Bible study series *Knowing the Bible*. The skilled authors and notable editors provide the contours of each book of the Bible as well as the grand theological themes that bind them together as one Book. Here, in a 12-week format, are carefully wrought studies that will ignite the mind and the heart."

> **R. KENT HUGHES,** Visiting Professor of Practical Theology, Westminster Theological Seminary

"*Knowing the Bible* brings together a gifted team of Bible teachers to produce a high-quality series of study guides. The coordinated focus of these materials is unique: biblical content, provocative questions, systematic theology, practical application, and the gospel story of God's grace presented all the way through Scripture."

> **PHILIP G. RYKEN,** President, Wheaton College

"These *Knowing the Bible* volumes provide a significant and very welcome variation on the general run of inductive Bible studies. This series provides substantial instruction, as well as teaching through the very questions that are asked. *Knowing the Bible* then goes even further by showing how any given text links with the gospel, the whole Bible, and the formation of theology. I heartily endorse this orientation of individual books to the whole Bible and the gospel, and I applaud the demonstration that sound theology was not something invented later by Christians, but is right there in the pages of Scripture."

> **GRAEME L. GOLDSWORTHY,** former lecturer, Moore Theological College; author, *According to Plan, Gospel and Kingdom, The Gospel in Revelation,* and *Gospel and Wisdom*

"What a gift to earnest, Bible-loving, Bible-searching believers! The organization and structure of the Bible study format presented through the *Knowing the Bible* series is so well conceived. Students of the Word are led to understand the content of passages through perceptive, guided questions, and they are given rich insights and application all along the way in the brief but illuminating sections that conclude each study. What potential growth in depth and breadth of understanding these studies offer! One can only pray that vast numbers of believers will discover more of God and the beauty of his Word through these rich studies."

> **BRUCE A. WARE,** Professor of Christian Theology, The Southern Baptist Theological Seminary

KNOWING THE BIBLE

J. I. Packer, Theological Editor
Dane C. Ortlund, Series Editor
Lane T. Dennis, Executive Editor

•   •   •   •   •   •

Genesis	Psalms	John	1–2 Thessalonians
Exodus	Proverbs	Acts	1–2 Timothy
Leviticus	Ecclesiastes	Romans	and Titus
Deuteronomy	Isaiah	1 Corinthians	Hebrews
Joshua	Jeremiah	2 Corinthians	James
Ruth and Esther	Daniel	Galatians	1–2 Peter
1–2 Kings	Hosea	Ephesians	and Jude
Ezra and	Matthew	Philippians	Revelation
Nehemiah	Mark	Colossians and	
Job	Luke	Philemon	

•   •   •   •   •   •

J. I. PACKER is Board of Governors' Professor of Theology at Regent College (Vancouver, BC). Dr. Packer earned his DPhil at the University of Oxford. He is known and loved worldwide as the author of the best-selling book *Knowing God*, as well as many other titles on theology and the Christian life. He serves as the General Editor of the ESV Bible and as the Theological Editor for the *ESV Study Bible*.

LANE T. DENNIS is President of Crossway, a not-for-profit publishing ministry. Dr. Dennis earned his PhD from Northwestern University. He is Chair of the ESV Bible Translation Oversight Committee and Executive Editor of the *ESV Study Bible*.

DANE C. ORTLUND is Executive Vice President of Bible Publishing and Bible Publisher at Crossway. He is a graduate of Covenant Theological Seminary (MDiv, ThM) and Wheaton College (BA, PhD). Dr. Ortlund has authored several books and scholarly articles in the areas of Bible, theology, and Christian living.

DEUTERONOMY

A 12-WEEK STUDY

Matthew H. Patton

WHEATON, ILLINOIS

To Daniel I. Block
Mentor, teacher, friend

Knowing the Bible: Deuteronomy, A 12-Week Study

Copyright © 2017 by Crossway

Published by Crossway
  1300 Crescent Street
  Wheaton, Illinois 60187

Some content used in this study guide has been adapted from the *ESV Study Bible* (Crossway), copyright 2008 by Crossway, pages 325–383. Used by permission. All rights reserved.

Cover design: Simplicated Studio

First printing 2017

Printed in the United States of America

Trade paperback ISBN: 978-1-4335-5378-3
EPub ISBN: 978-1-4335-5381-3
PDF ISBN: 978-1-4335-5379-0
Mobipocket ISBN: 978-1-4335-5380-6

Crossway is a publishing ministry of Good News Publishers.

VP		28	27	26	25	24	23	22	21	20	19	18	17
15	14	13	12	11	10	9	8	7	6	5	4	3	2	1

TABLE OF CONTENTS

SERIES PREFACE

KNOWING THE BIBLE, as the series title indicates, was created to help readers know and understand the meaning, the message, and the God of the Bible. Each volume in the series consists of 12 units that progressively take the reader through a clear, concise study of that book of the Bible. In this way, any given volume can fruitfully be used in a 12-week format either in group study, such as in a church-based context, or in individual study. Of course, these 12 studies could be completed in fewer or more than 12 weeks, as convenient, depending on the context in which they are used.

Each study unit gives an overview of the text at hand before digging into it with a series of questions for reflection or discussion. The unit then concludes by highlighting the gospel of grace in each passage ("Gospel Glimpses"), identifying whole-Bible themes that occur in the passage ("Whole-Bible Connections"), and pinpointing Christian doctrines that are affirmed in the passage ("Theological Soundings").

The final component to each unit is a section for reflecting on personal and practical implications from the passage at hand. The layout provides space for recording responses to the questions proposed, and we think readers need to do this to get the full benefit of the exercise. The series also includes definitions of key words. These definitions are indicated by a note number in the text and are found at the end of each chapter.

Lastly, to help understand the Bible in this deeper way, we urge readers to use the ESV Bible and the *ESV Study Bible*, which are available in various print and digital formats, including online editions at esv.org. The Knowing the Bible series is also available online. Additional 12-week studies covering each book of the Bible will be added as they become available.

May the Lord greatly bless your study as you seek to know him through knowing his Word.

J. I. Packer
Lane T. Dennis

WEEK 1: OVERVIEW

Deuteronomy (the title is Greek for "second law" or "second lawgiving") is a national constitution, a founding document for the new life that Israel is about to begin in the Land of Promise. Forty years previously, God had brought Israel out of bondage in Egypt and made a covenant[1] with them at Sinai. But then, instead of receiving the land God had promised to them, Israel refused to enter it and was compelled to wander in the wilderness for 40 years. Now, at the end of those 40 years, Israel is on the cusp of entering the land once more. The book of Deuteronomy is the great, all-encompassing vision for what life in the land should look like for God's people.

But Deuteronomy is also a farewell sermon. Moses is now 120 years old and is about to die. For decades he served as a mediator: he was God's messenger to Israel and represented Israel's requests to God. He was also Israel's ruler, guide, and judge, with authority unsurpassed by anyone else in Israel. As his monumental life draws to a close, Deuteronomy is Moses' last plea to Israel to live by the light of all that God has taught them.

And yet, Deuteronomy is ultimately about what *God* does for Israel, not what Israel does for God. The call to obedience (chs. 4–26) is rooted in God's redemptive work in the past (chs. 1–11) as well as the promise of God's work in the future (chs. 27–28). Even as Deuteronomy reckons with Israel's profound brokenness and inability to obey (chs. 29, 31–32), it still holds forth an unshakable hope for the future based on God's faithfulness (chs. 30, 32–33).

(For further background, see the *ESV Study Bible*, pages 325–329; also online at esv.org).

Placing Deuteronomy in the Larger Story

To begin to read Deuteronomy is to enter an epic story midstream. Deuteronomy is a major milestone in a narrative that began all the way back in Genesis and that continues to the end of Revelation.

Back in Genesis, God made several promises to Abraham: Abraham would have abundant offspring, this offspring would have a covenant relationship with God, and this offspring would enjoy that covenant relationship with God in the land of Canaan (Gen. 17:6–8). These promises encompass all that the garden of Eden held out to Adam before his fall into sin: a holy[2] God dwelling among a holy people in a holy place. What Adam forfeited, God promises he will still provide one day.

By the time we reach Deuteronomy, Abraham's offspring have become a large nation (Ex. 1:7; Deut. 1:10), and God has established his covenant with them at Sinai (Ex. 24:1–8). What remains is for them to enter the Promised Land, which they are about to do (see the book of Joshua). Deuteronomy calls Israel to the obedience that leads to genuine life with the Lord, in contrast to Adam's choice of death.

But Israel ultimately chooses death, just as Adam did, and they must be removed from the land (Judges–Kings). Thus Deuteronomy points forward to the true Adam and the true Israel, Jesus Christ. Jesus Christ obeyed God on our behalf and won for us the ultimate fulfillment of the promises to Abraham: eternal life. He thus brings about the holy kingdom foreshadowed in Deuteronomy.

Key Verse

"I call heaven and earth to witness against you today, that I have set before you life and death, blessing and curse. Therefore choose life, that you and your offspring may live, loving the LORD your God, obeying his voice and holding fast to him, for he is your life and length of days, that you may dwell in the land that the LORD swore to your fathers, to Abraham, to Isaac, and to Jacob, to give them." (Deut. 30:19–20)

Date and Historical Background

Deuteronomy records its own writing, stating in 31:9 that "Moses wrote this law and gave it to the priests, the sons of Levi, who carried the ark of the covenant of the LORD, and to all the elders of Israel" (see also 31:22, 24). In context, "this law" probably refers to most of the book, which Moses wrote shortly before his death in either 1406 or 1220 BC (see the *ESV Study Bible*, pages 33, 385 for further discussion). However, even though Moses was responsible for most of Deuteronomy, there are a few parts of the book that date from a later time. These include the framing words in 1:1–5 (with its reference to events "beyond the Jordan"), the account of Moses' death in chapter 34, and small editorial comments (e.g., 2:10–12). But as much as God may have seen fit to enhance Deuteronomy for later audiences, the core of the book was available in written form throughout Israel's history, both for their instruction (17:18; 31:10–13; 33:10) and as a witness against them when they disobeyed (31:19, 26).

Outline

  I. Prologue: Israel's Recent History (1:1–3:29)
    A. Setting of the book (1:1–5)
    B. Israel's failure at Kadesh-barnea (1:6–46)
    C. The journey to the plains of Moab (2:1–3:29)
 II. The Heart of Covenant Life with the Lord (4:1–11:32)
    A. The uniqueness of the Lord and his law (4:1–43)
    B. The Ten Commandments and Moses as mediator (4:44–5:33)
    C. Israel to obey the Lord alone (6:1–8:20)
       1. With all that they are (6:1–25)
       2. Not drawn away by other nations (7:1–26)
       3. Not boasting in themselves (8:1–20)
    D. Israel to love the Lord (9:1–11:32)
       1. For his grace shown at Sinai (9:1–10:11)
       2. For his powerful love to Israel (10:12–22)
       3. For the reward of life in the land (11:1–32)
III. Specific Commands (12:1–26:19)
    A. Concerning the place of worship (12:1–32)
    B. Concerning false teachers (13:1–18)
    C. Concerning food and times of the year (14:1–16:17)
    D. Concerning leaders, war, and justice (16:18–21:9)
    E. Concerning marriage, money, and the details of life (21:10–25:19)
    F. Concerning the firstfruits (26:1–19)
 IV. Blessings and Curses (27:1–29:1)
  V. The Future of Israel (29:2–33:29)
    A. God's implacable anger (29:2–29)
    B. A future beyond judgment (30:1–10)
    C. Moses' final plea (30:11–20)
    D. New leaders, but the certainty of Israel's apostasy (31:1–29)
    E. A song of Israel's future (31:30–32:52)
    F. Moses blesses Israel (33:1–29)
 VI. Epilogue: The Death of Moses (34:1–12)

As You Get Started

Before you began this study, what did you expect Deuteronomy to be about?

Does it seem strange that a book with so many laws could ultimately be about God's grace? If so, why?

List some questions you have about Deuteronomy. Perhaps some will have to do with how an ancient book written for Israel could apply to Christians today, which will be a central concern for this study.

As You Finish This Unit . . .

God gave the whole Old Testament to instill a hunger for Christ, the coming Redeemer of God's people. Ask God to help you approach Deuteronomy with an open heart, expectant that God will feed you here with his grace.

Definitions

[1] **Covenant** – A binding agreement between two parties, typically involving a formal statement of their relationship, a list of obligations for both parties, a list of witnesses to the agreement, and a list of curses for unfaithfulness and blessings for faithfulness to the agreement.

[2] **Holy** – Set apart by God for a good and special purpose.

Week 2: The Sins of the Fathers and the Faithfulness of God

Deuteronomy 1:1–3:29

▲

The Place of the Passage

The first three chapters of Deuteronomy situate the book within the epic story of the Bible. In the past 40 years, Israel has gone from Mount Sinai (known in Deuteronomy as "Horeb") up to the plains of Moab, just east of the Promised Land. But in between these two locations were 40 years of wilderness wandering, the result of Israel's failure to enter the land when they were first offered it at Kadesh-barnea. Now that God is offering Israel a second chance to enter the land, Moses shows what the past teaches them: Israel's previous refusal to enter the land was a heinous rebellion against God, motivated by fear and unbelief. The new generation will succeed where the previous generation failed only if they trust that God is both (1) still committed to his promise to give Israel the land and (2) able to keep this promise.

The Big Picture

In the face of fears about conquering the Promised Land, Israel must remember God's constant faithfulness and not repeat their fathers' sins.

Reflection and Discussion

Read through the complete passage for this study, Deuteronomy 1:1–3:29. Then review the following questions and record your responses. (For further background, see the *ESV Study Bible*, pages 330–336, or visit esv.org.)

1. The Command to Possess the Land (1:1–8)

Moses begins by recounting events 40 years prior to his writing, when Israel was still at Horeb (Mount Sinai). God commanded them to go up to the land that he had promised to Abraham more than 400 years before. What incentives does Moses give in these verses to motivate Israel for this journey?

2. A Growing Nation (1:9–18)

Even though Moses grieves at the burden the people have become (vv. 9, 12), what is encouraging about the people's great numbers? (Consider Deut. 1:10 in light of Gen. 15:5.)

3. The Failure at Kadesh-barnea (1:19–46)

Israel was offered the land by God, but they refused to enter. What specific reasons did they give for their refusal?

What was it about the failure of Israel at Kadesh-barnea that made this sin especially grievous? Be sure to note the further debacle in verses 41–46.

God responds to Israel's sin in a way that is simultaneously just (see vv. 34–40; note also the repetition of the word "listen" in vv. 43, 45) and yet also uncompromising in regard to his promise to give the land to Abraham's descendants. How does he achieve both purposes at the same time?

4. The End of Israel's Wandering (2:1–15)

After Israel's failure at Kadesh-barnea, this section quickly skips over the many years of wandering and recounts only the final stops in the lands of Edom (vv. 1–7) and Moab (vv. 8–15). Each of these nations had received their land from the Lord as a possession (vv. 5, 9), and they did so by first fighting off giants like the ones Israel will face in the Promised Land (vv. 10–12, 22; note also what is said about the "people of Ammon" in vv. 18–23). How do these stories of other nations encourage Israel?

5. The Beginning of the Conquest (2:16–3:17)

The kings Sihon and Og controlled territories to the north of Edom and Moab. Unlike Edom, Moab, and Ammon, whose ancestry derived from near relatives of Israel (from Esau and from Lot's children), these two kings were Amorite, a word synonymous with "Canaanite" in this context (3:8). They are therefore of the people group whom God promised to judge in due time (Gen. 15:16). The victories over these two kings follow a pattern: (1) God's command to take possession (Deut. 2:24–25, 31; 3:1–2); (2) the utter defeat of the enemy (2:32–33, 36; 3:3, 6); (3) the capture of the enemy's wealth (2:34–35; 3:4–5, 7); and (4) the giving of the conquered territories as permanent possessions to individual Israelite tribes (3:12–17). One of the Amorite kings is even a giant (Og; see 3:11). How does this recent history give Israel even more encouragement than they had at Kadesh-barnea?

Read through the following three sections on *Gospel Glimpses*, *Whole-Bible Connections*, and *Theological Soundings*. Then take time to consider the *Personal Implications* these sections may have for you.

Gospel Glimpses

PAST FAITHFULNESS, PRESENT HOPE. All of our hopes are riding on God's character, on whether he will be true to himself. As Israel wavers as to whether they will be successful in conquering the Promised Land, Moses directs their eyes to God and *his* faithfulness, not to Israel and their strength. In 1:30, Moses reminds Israel of how God fought for them in Egypt, which climaxed in the utter destruction of Pharaoh's army at the Red Sea. Moses reminds them of how God then provided for them in the wilderness: God carried them "as a man carries his son" (1:31), and for 40 years they lacked nothing (2:7). And most recently, as they have begun the conquest with the defeat of Kings Sihon and Og, they have seen with their own eyes the power of God to give them complete victory (2:31–3:11). Even when the Israelites themselves underwent judgment, as they did for their 40 years of wandering, they were encouraged by seeing that God keeps his word (2:14). To have hope for their present challenge, they must believe that God will continue to be faithful as he has been in the past. He has never given them a reason to think otherwise. In the same way, Christians derive genuine hope when we recall God's past faithfulness: "He who did not spare his own Son but gave him up for us all, how will he not also with him graciously give us all things?" (Rom. 8:32).

YOUR GOD FIGHTS FOR YOU. God does not promise merely to cooperate with Israel in their battles. He is the divine warrior who fights on Israel's behalf and wins the victory for them (1:30; 3:22; 20:4). When he fights for them, they have absolute certainty of success, and when he does not fight for them, the result is total failure (1:42–45). Thus, when Israel goes into battle, what matters is their trust in and obedience to the Lord, not their military might (20:8; Judg. 7:1–8; Ps. 20:7–8). In the same way, Christ comes as a warrior, singlehandedly vanquishing the powers of death and hell in his death and resurrection (Col. 2:13–15). Our victory over sin comes not from our own fighting prowess but by trusting Christ and entering into his victory by faith (Rom. 8:37).

Whole-Bible Connections

THE PROMISES TO THE FATHERS. God's promises to Abraham, Isaac, and Jacob loom large in Deuteronomy. These promises motivated God to initiate his saving work in the exodus from Egypt (Ex. 2:24), and he has already shown himself faithful to some of what he promised (e.g., making Israel as numerous as the stars in the heavens, as he promised to Abraham; Gen. 15:5; Deut. 1:10). Now his unfulfilled promises explain the great next steps he commands Israel to take. As we examine God's word to Abraham in Genesis 15:1–21, two major purposes must be accomplished: (1) Israel's possession of the land (Gen. 15:18; notice how Deut. 1:7 echoes this description), and (2) the judgment of the Amorites for their iniquity (Gen. 15:16). These two purposes will be accomplished simultaneously: by removing the Amorites, Israel will be able to possess the land. And yet, the timing is the Lord's: Israel can enter into blessing only when they are moving toward what God has promised (e.g., they cannot take the lands of Edom, Moab, or Ammon, which were not promised to them; see 2:5, 9, 19, 37) and only when God determines that the time is right. For Israel in Deuteronomy, the time of fulfillment is now at hand.

THE CHURCH POISED TO ENTER A NEW LAND. In the New Testament, the author of Hebrews identifies the church as being in a place very similar to Israel when they stood outside the land in Deuteronomy. Like Israel, we look to enter the rest that God promises to us, only this time the rest is even better than the

Promised Land: we seek a heavenly country (Heb. 4:9; 9:24). As with Israel, our ability to enter the land depends not on ourselves but on faith in God's provision (Heb. 4:2). But unlike Israel's situation, our mediator is not forbidden from entering (Deut. 3:26–27). Where Moses fell short, Christ succeeds. He is our forerunner and has already entered into our heavenly rest ahead of us, now beckoning us to follow in his footsteps (Heb. 4:14; 6:19–20).

Theological Soundings

REBELLION. Deuteronomy presents a robust and unsentimental view of sin. On the surface, sin presents itself as rebellion, such as Israel's refusal to enter the land when God commanded (1:26) and then their attempt to take the land when God condemned them to wander for 40 years (1:43). But sin is subtler than mere outward refusal to obey. Sin has its roots in unteachability, in a proud insistence that God is not who he says he is (1:27: "Because the LORD hated us he has brought us out of the land of Egypt"), and in an incapacity to listen to correction (1:43). And still deeper, sin springs from unbelief: the unwillingness to trust God's word and to believe that he is capable of giving what he has promised.

SOVEREIGNTY. Although the Lord has a special relationship with Israel, he remains the God of all creation. Even nations who do not worship him receive their respective lands from him (Edom, Moab, Ammon), and they can lose their lands at any time if the Lord wishes (as in the cases of Sihon king of Heshbon and Og king of Bashan). In contrast to the polytheistic view that the world is controlled by many different spiritual forces that are basically on the same level, Deuteronomy puts forward the Lord as the supreme unrivalled God of all things.

Personal Implications

Take some time to reflect on what you have learned from your study of Deuteronomy 1:1–3:29 and how it might apply to your own life today. Make notes below on the personal implications for your walk with the Lord of the (1) *Gospel Glimpses*, (2) *Whole-Bible Connections*, (3) *Theological Soundings*, and (4) this passage as a whole.

1. Gospel Glimpses

2. Whole-Bible Connections

3. Theological Soundings

4. Deuteronomy 1:1–3:29

As You Finish This Unit . . .

Take a moment now to ask for the Lord's blessing and help as you continue in this study of Deuteronomy. Then look back through this unit to reflect on key things the Lord may be teaching you.

WEEK 3: WHO IS LIKE THE LORD?

Deuteronomy 4:1–43

The Place of the Passage

Moses the preacher warms to his theme in Deuteronomy 4. With Israel's inconsistent past in view (chs. 1–3), Moses solemnly enjoins Israel to remember and keep what he has commanded them. Their very lives depend on it, as does their enjoyment of the land. To forget and disobey God's commands would not only compromise Israel's blessedness; it would also fly in the face of all that God is and all he has done for Israel. These crucial ideas—who God is, what he has done for Israel, and what Israel now is to do in response—are the great themes of the book, which this chapter weaves together. In so doing, it orients us to the overall message of Deuteronomy. For this reason we are dedicating a whole week's study to Deuteronomy chapter 4.

The Big Picture

Unlike any other god, the Lord has drawn near to Israel to save them and to reveal his law to them, and therefore they must be careful to keep his commands.

> ## Reflection and Discussion

Read through the complete passage for this study, Deuteronomy 4:1–43. Then review the following questions and record your responses. (For further background, see the *ESV Study Bible*, pages 337–339, or visit esv.org.)

1. Life and Death (4:1–4)

The great choice facing Israel is whether or not they will obey the Lord. Their loyalty to God is an either-or, take-it-or-leave-it decision. They cannot pick and choose what they like from God's law, or add other things they wish God had included (v. 2). What reasons do these verses give for why they should choose to obey God with all that they are? (For the background on "Baal of Peor," see Num. 25:1–9.)

2. A Great Nation (4:5–8)

Moses envisions Israel's keeping of God's commands. They even are given the title "great nation," fulfilling still another promise to Abraham (Gen. 12:2; 18:18; see "The Promises to the Fathers" in the "Whole-Bible Connections" section of Week 2). According to Deuteronomy 4:5–8, what about Israel is so great? What sets Israel apart from the rest of the nations?

3. Grace in the Past: God's Revelation at Sinai (4:9–14)

Verse 9 is the first of three times that Moses warns Israel to "take care" (see also vv. 15, 23). What spiritual traps is Moses concerned that Israel will fall into, as described in verses 9–14?

Amid the terror of "darkness, cloud, and gloom" (v. 11) are several statements of purpose that reveal God's grace at work (see the three uses of "that" in v. 10; see also v. 14). How do these statements show his grace?

4. The Danger of Idolatry (4:15–24)

God permits Israel to see many things (the phrase "your eyes have seen" is repeated in 3:21; 4:3, 9; 10:21; 11:7; 29:2), but he does not let them see himself. And yet, even as God shrouds himself in fire and cloud, he reveals something. What do God's refusal to be seen (v. 15) and his refusal to be represented by visible things (vv. 16–19, 23) reveal about his uniqueness?

5. Grace in the Future (4:25–31)

God is uncompromising in his judgment (vv. 25–28) but also in his mercy (vv. 29–31). Even if God removed Israel from the land in judgment, Israel would still have hope for a future. What must Israel do to receive this mercy (see v. 29)? Why would God give it (see v. 31)?

6. No One like the Lord (4:32–40)

The confession that the Lord alone is God is the great rallying cry of Deuteronomy (vv. 35, 39; see also 6:4). It is the first thing true faith confesses (see Josh. 2:11; 22:34; 1 Kings 8:60; 18:39). According to this section, how was Israel to recognize that this core claim is true?

Read through the following three sections on *Gospel Glimpses, Whole-Bible Connections,* and *Theological Soundings.* Then take time to consider the *Personal Implications* these sections may have for you.

Gospel Glimpses

REVEALED RELIGION. Simply to know God is a gracious gift. The nations are reduced to speculation about what their gods desire, whether they are pleasing to their gods, and what the future holds (Jer. 10:5; Jonah 4:11). But Israel gets to hear God's voice from the fire (Deut. 4:36) and through the preaching of his faithful messenger, Moses (4:1). Israel should marvel at having a God so near (4:7), a God who makes himself known so clearly to his people (see 30:11–14). Indeed, even after God ceases to appear in fire on Sinai, he is still near his people through the written Word. This close identification between God and his written Word explains the command neither to add nor to subtract from his words (4:2; see 12:32; Rev. 22:18–19), for his written Word represents him and his authority. But even better than this written Word is the very climax of God's gracious revelation, Jesus Christ: "The Word became flesh and dwelt among us, and we have seen his glory, glory as of the only Son from the Father, full of grace and truth" (John 1:14). In Christ, God's Word has graciously come near us, not merely in written words but as a human being.

ENDURING FAITHFULNESS. Verses 29–31 of Deuteronomy 4 astonish us with their description of God's enduring mercy. Even after Israel will sin grievously and God's righteous anger will come upon them to scatter them among the peoples, they will still have hope. This hope is rooted in God's tremendous compassion, for he is moved by the misery of his people, even when it is self-inflicted (v. 31; see Neh. 9:17, 19, 27, 28, 31). And their hope is rooted also in God's faithfulness to his ancient promises to Abraham, Isaac, and Jacob (Deut. 4:31). When all the initial fulfillments of these promises are removed by God's judgment (when they are removed from their land, and are left few in number), God says he will *still* remember what he promised to Abraham. In the work of Christ, God's promised compassion and faithfulness have arrived. Christ comes to fulfill the promises made to Abraham (Luke 1:72–73; Gal. 3:29). And in Christ, God compassionately receives his scattered people as the father receives the Prodigal Son (Luke 15:20). Judgment has given way to reconciliation and resurrection.

Whole-Bible Connections

CREATION RIGHTLY ORDERED. The language of Deuteronomy 4:16–19 is filled with recollections of Genesis 1: the lists of creatures ("animal . . . on the earth," "winged bird," "fish," things that "creep on the ground"), the list of heavenly bodies ("sun," "moon," and "stars"), and the important concept of "form" or "likeness." These verses in Deuteronomy 4 recall the well-ordered world God made, and they apply this picture to the realm of worship: the biblical pattern is that God makes his own image (Gen. 1:26–28). He is the archetype and template for all creation, infinitely higher than all he has made. We are copies and pictures of him. Hence we must not claim for ourselves the right to make likenesses of God (pictures, statues, etc.; see Deut. 4:16, 23), as though *we* were *his* creator and could manipulate him. Part of honoring this creational order is respecting the difference between males and females. Using the same language as Genesis 1 and Deuteronomy 4:16–19, Romans 1:18–27 describes the perversion of all humanity, not just in our rejection of God in favor of images that we construct but also in our tendency to reject the basic creational distinction between males and females.

IDOLATRY'S TREACHERY. Faithfulness to God's covenant is like the faithfulness of a wife to her husband. Hence the faithful Israelites at Baal-peor were those who did not go after idols or sexual immorality but "held fast" (or "clung") to the Lord (v. 4; for the marital overtones of this word, see Gen. 2:24; Josh. 23:12). God is steadfastly dedicated to Israel and treasures her as his own inheritance (Deut. 4:20; 26:18). As in any dedicated marriage, God rightly expects Israel to return his fidelity, which in this case means worshiping him exclusively (4:19). This desire for exclusive worship is like the jealousy of a husband: the Lord is a "jealous God" (v. 24). In light of all that God has done for Israel and the explicit command he gives here, it comes as a knife thrust to read the same language repeated later in Israel's history: "They abandoned all the commandments of the LORD their God, and made for themselves *metal images* of two calves; and they made an Asherah and worshiped *all the host of heaven* and served Baal" (2 Kings 17:16).

> **Theological Soundings**

THE UNIQUENESS OF GOD. All of the commands in Deuteronomy stem from the Lord's being different from every other so-called "god." Verses 32–34 of Deuteronomy 4 drive home the uniqueness of the Lord with three powerful questions: Has any other event like the salvation of Israel from Egypt ever happened (v. 32)? Has any other people ever heard the voice of God and lived (v. 33)? Has any other god taken a people for himself from the midst of another nation through great wonders (v. 34)? The answer in every case is a resounding no! No such event! No such people! No such other god! The "gods" of all the other nations are paralyzed: they can "neither see, nor hear, nor eat, nor smell" (v. 28). As Jeremiah mocks, they "cannot do evil, neither is it in them to do good" (Jer. 10:5). The only things the Lord "cannot" do are leaving, destroying, or forgetting Israel (Deut. 4:31). This unique relationship between Israel and their unique God is not a reason for boasting, as though they were any better than the other nations or inherently more deserving than them (4:37; 7:7; 9:5). Rather, it demands their exclusive worship and devotion.

Personal Implications

Take some time to reflect on what you have learned from your study of Deuteronomy 4:1–43 and how it might apply to your own life today. Make notes below on the personal implications for your walk with the Lord of the (1) *Gospel Glimpses*, (2) *Whole-Bible Connections*, (3) *Theological Soundings*, and (4) this passage as a whole.

1. Gospel Glimpses

2. Whole-Bible Connections

3. Theological Soundings

4. Deuteronomy 4:1–43

As You Finish This Unit . . .

Take a moment now to ask for the Lord's blessing and help as you continue in this study of Deuteronomy. Then look back through this unit to reflect on key things the Lord may be teaching you.

WEEK 4: LOVE THE LORD

Deuteronomy 4:44–6:9

▲

The Place of the Passage

With Deuteronomy 1:1–4:43 as a historical and theological orientation, Moses begins a new section at Deuteronomy 4:44 that will continue all the way to 26:19, in which he calls Israel to obedience. He starts at the very heart of what it means to follow the Lord alone: Israel must love him with *all* that they are (6:5), and they are to express this love by keeping the Ten Commandments (5:7–21). Moses' pastoral exhortations for Israel to embody this basic attitude of loving obedience will occupy him for the next six chapters (chs. 6–11). Then he will give a detailed exposition of what it means to keep the Ten Commandments in all of life (chs. 12–26).

The Big Picture

Israel must love the Lord with all that they are by obeying the commands he has given through Moses.

> ## Reflection and Discussion

Read through the complete passage for this study, Deuteronomy 4:44–6:9. Then review the following questions and record your responses. (For further background, see the *ESV Study Bible*, pages 339–342, or visit esv.org.)

1. The Preface to God's Commands (4:44–49; 5:6)

Before any specific word is spoken in this section about what Israel must do, Moses speaks of what God has done for Israel. In 4:44–49 and 5:6, what specific acts of God are called to mind, and how would this background encourage Israel to keep God's commands?

2. The Ten Commandments (5:7–21)

Each of these laws protects something precious (e.g., v. 17 guards a person's life from being taken unjustly). List the interests protected in each of the laws. Reflect on what these protections reveal about sin's tendencies and God's priorities.

Several clues indicate that God is not interested merely in external conformity to his law (for confirmation of this, see Matt. 5:21–30). One of the Ten Commandments explicitly addresses our desires (Deut. 5:21), and several commands include motivations for obedience, both positive (vv. 10, 14, 15, 16) and negative (vv. 9, 11). What are these motivations, and what do they reveal about a heart rightly attuned to God's will?

3. Moses as Mediator (5:1–5, 22–33)

In verses 5 and 23–27 we see the fear-motivated request by Israel's elders for Moses to ascend the mountain. Exodus 19:16–19 and 20:18 vividly describe the awesome circumstances that led to this request. What does this fearful experience reveal about God's character?

Given their self-protective motives, we are surprised that God approves the people's request to have Moses as their mediator (vv. 28–29). God later echoes this approval by establishing future prophets as mediators (18:15–19). What does the Lord applaud about Israel's request?

5. The Greatest Commandment (6:1–5)

The ESV text ("The Lord our God, the Lord is one") and footnote ("The Lord our God is one Lord"; "THE Lord is our God, the Lord is one"; "The Lord is

WEEK 4: LOVE THE LORD

our God, the LORD alone") provide alternative translations for 6:4. The under-lying Hebrew words could legitimately support any of these translations. Since the translation of this verse cannot be resolved by the words alone, we must assess which translation fits best in context. Try each translation in context, and evaluate which best supports the flow of thought.

Loving the Lord with all our *heart*, with all our *soul*, and with all our *might* (v. 5) leaves nothing out. Our whole lives must be devoted to the Lord: our thoughts and desires, our actions, our skills and talents, and our time, possessions, and relationships. How do the Ten Commandments in the previous chapter reflect the life-encompassing quality of this great command?

6. A Life Centered on God's Word (6:6–9)

The command to love God goes hand-in-hand with loving his Word. The Word is to be impressed on our hearts like impressions on a clay tablet (v. 6; see Prov. 3:3; 7:3). It is to be on our lips in everyday life (v. 7). The commands in verses 8–9 about "signs," "frontlets," and writings on "doorposts" and "gates" suggest that the Word is to adorn our lives like precious jewelry kept close at all times or like decorations prominently displayed (Ex. 28:29, 36–38; Song 8:6). What attitudes about God's Word are assumed by these commands?

Read through the following three sections on *Gospel Glimpses, Whole-Bible Connections*, and *Theological Soundings*. Then take time to consider the *Personal Implications* these sections may have for you.

Gospel Glimpses

GRACE, THEN OBEDIENCE. The order of Israel's history reflects a profound truth about the gospel. As Deuteronomy 5:6 reminds us, God saves Israel *first* and *then* summons them to Sinai so that they can be instructed about how to obey his commands. Israel does not obey God *so that* they can enter a relationship with him; they already *are* in covenant with him. Later in Deuteronomy, God emphatically states that the blessings Israel enjoys are not because they obeyed him so well: "Know, therefore, that the LORD your God is not giving you this good land to possess because of your righteousness, for you are a stubborn people" (9:6). Indeed, God blesses them in spite of their sin! This gracious attitude is one that God pledges to maintain (see 4:29–31). And so he does, for the same basic structure of "grace, then obedience" lies at the heart of the gospel of Jesus Christ and even forms the template for several New Testament letters (e.g., Ephesians 1–3 and Romans 1–11 emphasize the finished work of Christ, and then Ephesians 4–6 and Romans 12–16 speak of how we must live in light of that finished work).

JESUS, THE BETTER MEDIATOR. Moses' role as mediator is central to Deuteronomy 5 and runs as a thread through the book. Juxtaposing 5:4 and 5:5, we can say that Israel is "face to face" with God (5:4) even though Moses stands between God and Israel, for, in a representative sense, Moses *is* Israel to God. Likewise, Moses represents God to Israel, for God speaks to Moses, who then relays God's words to Israel (5:27). The effect is that Moses' words are equated with God's words (1:3; 4:2), such that Israel will be held accountable for disobeying Moses' words as though they had disobeyed God himself (see 18:18–19). Yet for all of Moses' effectiveness as the mediator of the old covenant, Jesus far surpasses him as the mediator of the new (1 Tim. 2:5; Heb. 8:6; 9:15; 12:24). Jesus actually *is* God and man: for us to see him is to see the Father (John 14:9), and when the Father welcomes him, he welcomes all those whom Christ represents (Rom. 5:2). Jesus is our direct link to the Father, and the Father's link to us (John 14:23).

Whole-Bible Connections

ALL THE HEART AND ALL THE SOUL. The demand that Israel offer to God their *whole* heart, soul, and might is powerful language echoed throughout

Scripture, especially at times when Israel is reminded of their duty to God (Josh. 22:5; 1 Kings 2:4; 2 Kings 23:3; 2 Chron. 15:12; Matt. 22:37). Often shortened to "all the heart and all the soul," this catchphrase reminds us that God demands our *whole* selves, which is precisely what he deserves.

BIBLICAL LOVE. When Deuteronomy speaks of human love for God, it uses terms like "fear," "walk in God's ways," "serve," "hold fast," "obey," and "keep his commandments and statutes" (see 10:12–13; 11:1, 22; 19:9; 30:20). Love is virtually a synonym for "loyalty." In short, Jesus is saying nothing new when he says, "If you love me, you will keep my commandments" (John 14:15). Indeed, to have perfect love for God and for neighbor is to fulfill *all* of the law's commands (Matt. 22:40). We show our love for God when we obey him above every other demand or desire, including the demands of family (Deut. 13:3). Despite the closeness of familial love, it is to be like hatred in comparison to our love for God (Luke 14:26). Unfortunately, as we will see, Israel will fail God's repeated tests to determine whether their love for him is paramount, and it will be only in the time of the new covenant that our hearts will be renewed so that we can obey and love God above all others (Deut. 30:6).

Theological Soundings

CROSS-GENERATIONAL UNITY. Deuteronomy 5:3 alerts us to a key idea of the book: "Not with our fathers did the LORD make this covenant, but with us, who are all of us here alive today." Since the original audience of Moses' sermons was the children of the wilderness generation, many in this audience had not even been born when Israel was at Sinai some 40 years before. What, then, can Moses mean by "all of us"? The answer is that the Israel of a later generation is *one* with the previous generations and with those yet to come. For this reason, Moses can say that this present generation was "there" when God worked mightily for Israel in the past (e.g., 1:20, 29–31; 4:10, 15; 11:2–7). They are even considered eyewitnesses of those events (1:30; 11:7; 29:2–3)! As a result, they and all those who will descend from them are bound to obey the covenant, just as the first generation at Sinai was (5:32–33; 29:13–15). They also have as much a right to the promises as their forefathers did, and in the children receiving God's fulfillment of the promises it is as though the forefathers themselves have received them.

KEEPING THE LAW AS CHRISTIANS. As some of the first concrete rules Moses teaches, the Ten Commandments raise the crucial issue of how we as new covenant Christians should relate to the old covenant laws given in Deuteronomy. On the one hand, many laws refer to old covenant realities that no longer apply to us directly (e.g., the promise that "it may go well with [them] in *the land that the Lord your God is giving [them]*" if they honor their parents; Deut. 5:16). On the other hand, many laws are explicitly reaffirmed as expressions of God's moral will for Christians in the new covenant (e.g., not murdering or committing adultery; 1 Tim. 1:8–11). The question can be resolved only by first considering our relationship to the old covenant: as Christians, we are no longer "under" the old covenant, since it has been replaced by the new (Eph. 2:14–15; Heb. 8:13). But the old covenant remains the authoritative Word of God and is rich with insight into God's moral character. Each law must therefore be considered in turn, asking about both continuity and discontinuity. How do we see God's unchanging character reflected in this law? And how does the work of Christ change the way in which we are now bound to reflect God's character? Future lessons will explore this complex issue.

▶ Personal Implications

Take some time to reflect on what you have learned from your study of Deuteronomy 4:44–6:9 and how it might apply to your own life today. Make notes below on the personal implications for your walk with the Lord of the (1) *Gospel Glimpses*, (2) *Whole-Bible Connections*, (3) *Theological Soundings*, and (4) this passage as a whole.

1. Gospel Glimpses

2. Whole-Bible Connections

31

3. Theological Soundings

4. Deuteronomy 4:44–6:9

> ## As You Finish This Unit . . .

Take a moment now to ask for the Lord's blessing and help as you continue in this study of Deuteronomy. Then look back through this unit to reflect on key things the Lord may be teaching you.

WEEK 5: TESTS OF FAITH

Deuteronomy 6:10–8:20

▲

The Place of the Passage

God's law centers on the command to love him with all that we are (6:5). Before Moses outlines the details of loving God in all of life (chs. 12–26), he must first challenge the core attitudes of Israel's heart. Moses here warns the people of several great temptations that await them in the Promised Land, which will test their love for the Lord: tests of prosperity, forgetfulness, idolatry, covetousness, pride, and ingratitude. In each case Israel's very identity is at stake: if they fail the tests, they will forfeit everything God won for them when he saved them from Egypt.

The Big Picture

Israel must not forget who they are as God's people, rendering him thanks for the land's blessings, teaching their youth, and refusing to follow in the idolatry of the nations around them.

Reflection and Discussion

Read through the complete passage for this study, Deuteronomy 6:10–8:20. Then review the following questions and record your responses. (For further background, see the *ESV Study Bible*, pages 342–345, or visit esv.org.)

1. The Test of Riches (6:10–19)

Moses exhorts Israel not to test the Lord as they did at Massah (v. 16). At that time, Israel was deep in the wilderness, lacking water, and on the verge of death. They tested God by doubting his care for them (Ex. 17:1–7). How is the test Israel will face in the land different from the one they faced in the wilderness? How is it similar? (See especially vv. 10–15; compare Prov. 30:8–9.)

2. Teach Your Children (6:20–25)

The son's question in verse 20 reflects a teachable interest in the Lord. But the language also suggests that the son is still uncommitted to the Lord: he can speak of the Lord as "our God," yet he goes on to say that the commands were made to "you," suggesting the son does not yet fully identify himself with his father and with all Israel. The son does not say that the Lord commanded "us," as Deuteronomy 5:2 instructs future generations to do (see the section in last week's lesson about the "Cross-Generational Unity" of Israel). How does the father's reply in verses 21–25 wisely enfold his son into what it means to be a part of Israel?

3. Destroy the Nations (7:1–5, 16)

These verses are some of the most disturbing in the whole Bible, and the questions they raise will be discussed below under the heading "The Just Destruction of God's Enemies," in "Theological Soundings." For now, note carefully (1) what exactly the Lord is commanding Israel to do, and (2) what reasons he gives for these commands.

4. A Holy People, Blessed for Obedience (7:6–15)

This passage affirms God's gracious choice of Israel, a choice that he made without regard to Israel's worthiness (v. 6). God also reaffirms his promise that he will not withdraw his choice of Abraham and his offspring, even after many generations (vv. 8–9). Yet this special status does not imply favoritism on God's part, as though Israel were held to lighter standards of righteousness than the nations. How does this passage reinforce that obedience is the *only* path to blessing?

5. The Lord Is a Warrior (7:17–26)

Moses returns to the core issue facing Israel at this moment: their fear of military defeat before the nations in the Promised Land (v. 17; compare 1:28). Trace how Moses argues against this fear in verses 18–24. Remember that prior to the exodus,[1] Egypt was considered a superpower compared to the petty kingdoms of the Promised Land, and yet God defeated even Egypt.

6. From Wasteland to Wealth (8:1–10)

The generation about to enter the land could wrongly view their time of wandering in the wilderness as God's punishment for their sin. In fact, the punishment was on the previous generation, who died in the wilderness, and God intended in time to bring great blessing on the current generation (vv. 7–10; 1:39). But first there were several redemptive lessons the wilderness should have taught them. What were those lessons?

7. Lest You Forget (8:11–20)

For Israel, "forgetting" in this passage is more than amnesia; it is willfully embracing their pride and the lies they tell themselves in their hearts. What are the specific lies Israel will be tempted to speak to themselves? How does Moses rebuke those lies?

Read through the following three sections on *Gospel Glimpses, Whole-Bible Connections,* and *Theological Soundings.* Then take time to consider the *Personal Implications* these sections may have for you.

Gospel Glimpses

JESUS THE TRUE SON. These chapters contain the three texts Jesus quotes when he is tempted by Satan (Deut. 6:13, 16; 8:3). As Israel wandered 40 years in the wilderness, being tested by God, Jesus wandered 40 days in the wilderness, facing similar temptations to disobey God through food, testing God, and false worship (Matt. 4:1–11; Luke 4:1–13). And yet, where Israel failed, Jesus succeeded. In this way, Jesus showed himself to be the truly obedient son, whose heart is completely devoted to the Lord and whose righteousness brings blessing.

SLAVES SET FREE. Time and again, Deuteronomy looks back to the exodus from Egypt as the great event of Israel's past. When a father seeks to tell his son the core of who they are as Israelites, he focuses on how the Lord redeemed them from bondage by his great power (6:21–25). When Moses wants to remind the people of the Lord's love, he centers on the exodus (7:8). When they fear being defeated and subdued again by other nations, the exodus gives them hope (7:18). As long as Israel remembers that they are objects of grace, former slaves who are now set free, they will never give in to the boast that they are self-made men (8:17). In an even deeper way, Christians are slaves now set free, participants in a new and better exodus. For us in the new covenant, the great saving event was when Christ the Passover lamb offered his blood as the ransom price so that we would no longer be slaves of sin but would be free to obey God from the heart (Rom. 6:17–18; 1 Cor. 5:7; Titus 2:14).

BY GRACE. The previous two Gospel Glimpses provide the proper context for understanding the role of good works in Deuteronomy. The statement that it "will be righteousness" for Israel if they are "careful to do" all that the Lord has commanded (Deut. 6:25) seems, on the surface, to be advocating works-righteousness. The idea that we are righteous because of what we do is the antithesis of the Reformation's insistence that salvation is by grace alone through faith alone. But we know that the same Spirit who inspired Moses to write this verse is the one who inspired Paul to write passages like Ephesians 2:4–10 and Titus 3:3–7, which emphasize our being saved apart from works. In this light, the promise that Israel's obedience will be "righteousness" is not referring to their meriting salvation, since they are already saved (see "Slaves Set Free," above). Nor is their obedience considered "righteousness" in the perfect, absolute sense, which we see only in Christ (see "Jesus the True Son," above). Rather, "righteousness" is used more loosely here to refer to a life of faith in God's promises that bears fruit in faithful obedience and leads to blessing in the land (Deut. 8:1).

Whole-Bible Connections

TEACHING THE NEXT GENERATION. The rise of each new generation of Israelites poses a new challenge. If the older generation does not pass on what they have learned, Israel will forget all that they are. Hence Moses warns repeatedly about forgetfulness (4:9, 23; 6:12; 8:11, 14, 19; 9:7). Indeed, forgetfulness is the road to apostasy: forgetfulness leads to a lack of gratitude, which in turn leads to self-reliant boasting (8:11–18; see Rom. 1:21–23). The antidote to forgetfulness is diligent teaching, which is commanded in 6:6–9 and modeled in

6:20–25. Unfortunately, the very generation that Moses addresses fails in this all-important command, and we read with horror in Judges 2:10 that "All that generation [the original audience of Deuteronomy] also were gathered to their fathers. And there arose another generation after them who did not know the LORD or the work that he had done for Israel." Many times thereafter in Israel we see godly men followed by godless sons.

Theological Soundings

THE JUST DESTRUCTION OF GOD'S ENEMIES. Zeal for justice is a good and upright part of God's character: as the holy judge, he is a "consuming fire" (Deut. 4:24; 9:3), jealous for truth. And yet, unlike human anger, which so often lashes out in disproportionate severity, God's justice is always measured and righteous (32:4; Ps. 9:8). This truth is the path to understanding the command in Deuteronomy 7:1–5 to destroy the Canaanites. As Deuteronomy 18:9–12 and Leviticus 18–19 catalog, the Canaanites were deep in the appalling sins of child sacrifice, sexual immorality, witchcraft, and idolatry, all of which are sins worthy of God's holy anger. What is more, God gave them ample time to repent, and some even did (Gen. 15:16; Josh. 2:8–13). God does not sadistically delight to judge but rather calls all to repentance (Ezek. 33:11). Yet he will not hold back his judgment forever. And even if God graciously chose to save and forgive some (Rom. 9:21), one cannot call the destruction of the Canaanites an act of racist genocide, for God later inflicts the same punishment on his own people when they do worse than the Canaanites did (2 Kings 21:11–12). In the New Testament we see that God's judgments in the Old Testament are but shadows of a much greater judgment to come. Far from there being an Old Testament God of wrath in contrast with a New Testament God of love, the true God of the Bible is both just and loving and is reserving his greatest outpouring of wrath for the last great day (Rev. 19:11–21). Indeed, God even came in the flesh to take this just wrath on *himself* for the sake of his people. While this affirmation of the justice of God does not answer all the questions of this troubling passage, it points a way for us to trust that God *is* good and *does* good—always (Ps. 119:68).

Personal Implications

Take some time to reflect on what you have learned from your study of Deuteronomy 6:10–8:20 and how it might apply to your own life today. Make notes below on the personal implications for your walk with the Lord of the (1) *Gospel Glimpses*, (2) *Whole-Bible Connections*, (3) *Theological Soundings*, and (4) this passage as a whole.

1. Gospel Glimpses

2. Whole-Bible Connections

3. Theological Soundings

4. Deuteronomy 6:10–8:20

As You Finish This Unit . . .

Take a moment now to ask for the Lord's blessing and help as you continue in this study of Deuteronomy. Then look back through this unit to reflect on key things the Lord may be teaching you.

Definition

[1] **Exodus** – The time when God brought Israel out of bondage in Egypt.

WEEK 6: A LAND GIVEN BY GRACE

Deuteronomy 9:1–11:32

The Place of the Passage

Moses has saved for last the two biggest spiritual tests that will challenge Israel's relationship with the Lord. The first concerns Israel's view of themselves: If they defeat the Canaanites, does that mean Israel is more righteous than they? Lest they fall prey to this thinking, Moses confronts them with their stubbornness (9:1–10:11). The second test concerns Israel's view of God: Will they forget all that he has done for them and give their hearts to other gods? In 10:12–11:32 Moses urges them to break with their past stubbornness and give their hearts wholly to the God who has so generously loved them.

The Big Picture

Instead of making empty boasts about their righteousness, Israel should recall their past sins with grief, dedicating themselves to wholehearted obedience so that they might enjoy the land God is giving them.

> ## Reflection and Discussion

Read through the complete passage for this study, Deuteronomy 9:1–11:32. Then review the following questions and record your responses. (For further background, see the *ESV Study Bible*, pages 345–349, or visit esv.org.)

1. Delusions of Grandeur (9:1–5)

For the third time, Moses challenges something that Israel might say "in their hearts" (9:4; compare 7:17; 8:17). The attention to these internal thought patterns shows God's concern for Israel's hearts. What is the lie Israel might be tempted to embrace after their victory over the nations in the land, and how does God correct this error?

2. Remember the Past (9:6–12)

"It is because of my righteousness that the LORD has brought me in to possess this land" (9:4). The absurdity of this boast is obvious when Moses reminds the Israelites of the golden calf incident. The full story is given in Exodus 32. What about this sin was so egregious? (See especially Deuteronomy 9:12; compare Exodus 24:3.)

3. Moses' Intercession (9:13–21)

The Lord's threat of annihilating Israel must have been very appealing to Moses (see Num. 11:11–15), as was the offer to start a new people with him (Deut.

42

9:14). But instead of accepting the offer, Moses performs a series of actions to avert God's wrath (see especially vv. 17–21). What are these actions, and what do they show about Moses' character?

_____

_____

_____

_____

4. Moses' Prayer (9:25–29)

Here we see the content of Moses' intercession. He makes no attempt to minimize Israel's sin or their deserving of God's anger, but nevertheless he gives several reasons why God must not destroy Israel. What are these reasons?

_____

_____

_____

_____

At the heart of Moses' plea is an insistence that Israel is still God's people (compare "your people" in Moses' mouth [v. 26] with "your people" and "this people" in the Lord's mouth [vv. 12, 13]). Based on the reasons listed in the previous response, how is Israel still God's people, even when they sin?

_____

_____

_____

_____

5. Starting Again (10:1–11)

Even though the Lord gives no direct reply to Moses, there are several indications in this text that Moses' prayer has been answered, not only for the people in general but also for Aaron and his house (see 9:20). Where in this passage do you see evidence of God's grace toward Aaron and the people?

_____

_____

_____

_____

6. Remember the Past (10:12–22)

There is perhaps no better collection of "command" words in Deuteronomy than in this section ("keep," "love," etc.). List all of the commands Moses gives in this passage. How do they give a full-orbed description of what it means to be loyal to God?

_____

_____

_____

_____

_____

All of these commands are given for good reasons (e.g., 10:19: "Love the sojourner, therefore, for you were sojourners in the land of Egypt"). The most fundamental reason for each command is God's character. List the things Moses says about the Lord in this section. How does God's character motivate obedience?

_____

_____

_____

_____

_____

_____

7. The Blessing and the Curse (11:1–32)

As Moses brings to a close his great exhortation to love the Lord, he confronts Israel with the urgent life-or-death decision that they face (see especially v. 26). Chapter 11 alternates between the life offered if they obey and the death threatened if they disobey. The offer of life is described in verses 8–15 and 18–25 and focuses on the Promised Land. What is so good about the land God is giving? How is it the epitome of the good life?

_____

_____

_____

_____

_____

In contrast, Moses threatens death in verses 1–7 and 16–17. He makes the threat explicit in verses 16–17, but in verses 1–7 he recalls the deaths that have already befallen God's enemies as a warning to Israel. What do these threats convey about God's attitude toward sin?

Read through the following three sections on *Gospel Glimpses, Whole-Bible Connections,* and *Theological Soundings.* Then take time to consider the *Personal Implications* these sections may have for you.

Gospel Glimpses

JESUS THE MEDIATOR. In chapter 9 Moses recalls how the Lord offered him a chance to be rid of the people whose grumblings had so provoked him to anger and despair. God even offered him the chance to be the head of a new people, who would be named after him (9:14). Yet he does not accept the Lord's offer, instead choosing a much harder route of fasting and prayer—for an additional 40 days (9:18)! His prayer in verses 26–29 shows that his passion for the Lord's reputation among the nations and his zeal for the Lord's fidelity to his promises far outweighs Moses' own aspirations for glory and honor. This same heart is seen in even greater majesty in the Lord Jesus Christ, our intercessor. When faced with the cross, he prays, "Now is my soul troubled. And what shall I say? 'Father, save me from this hour'? But for this purpose I have come to this hour. Father, *glorify your name*" (John 12:27–28). And today, because his zeal for the Father's glory drove him to the cross, he is presently praying that the Father would not regard our sin (see Deut. 9:27) but that the benefits of the cross might be ours instead (Rom. 8:34; Heb. 7:24).

THE LAND GIVEN IN SPITE OF ISRAEL. Deuteronomy 9:5–10:12 answers one key question: why does Israel get to enjoy the Promised Land? The Israelites flatter themselves with the lie that it is because they are so righteous, as though they deserved the land (9:4). But Moses bluntly contradicts this delusion. The real reason for their receiving the land is that the nations who previously occupied it woefully deserved judgment, and God had graciously promised the land to Israel's forefathers (Abraham, Isaac, and Jacob) long ago (9:5). But

Moses dedicates the bulk of his words (9:6–24) to showcasing Israel's horrific sin. If they deserved anything, it was judgment (see 11:16–17)! When the Lord graciously acquiesces in 10:1–12 to continue the journey toward the land, we realize it is not *because of* Israel that they receive the land but *in spite of* them. This is grace—to receive blessing when they instead deserved death. Christians receive their inheritance by the same principle: we were dead in the trespasses and sins in which we once walked (Eph. 2:1–2), but God made us alive in Christ all the same (Eph. 2:5): "*By grace* you have been saved through faith" (Eph. 2:8).

Whole-Bible Connections

LAND. The Old Testament spends a lot of time talking about the Promised Land. Inheritance of this land is one of the most important promises God made to Abraham (Gen. 12:7; 13:15; 15:18; 17:8), and as we have already seen several times in Deuteronomy, this land promise continues to drive God's gracious dealings toward Israel (Deut. 1:8; 9:5; 10:11). What becomes of the land promise in the New Testament? How does Jesus, who came to fulfill the promises to Abraham (Luke 1:73; Gal. 3:14), fulfill this all-important promise? The answer becomes clear when we consider how the New Testament speaks of the inheritance Christ has won for his people. The heirs of Abraham are those who have the faith of Abraham, whether Jew or Gentile[1] (Rom. 4:11–12; Gal. 3:29). This new covenant people of God receives nothing less than eternal life in the entire new creation: the new heavens and the new earth (Matt. 25:34; Rom. 4:13; Titus 3:7; Rev. 21:1–3)! They are coheirs with Christ, who has received all things from his Father (Matt. 28:18; Rom. 8:17; Eph. 1:22). As it happens, this better inheritance is what Abraham himself was seeking all along (Heb. 11:10, 16). One can hardly accuse God of failing to deliver on his promise when he has gone so far above and beyond what he originally said: the ultimate, new covenant people of God receive not a portion of the *old* creation but the entirety of the *new* creation! God loves to "hyper-fulfill" (go above and beyond) his ancient promises.

Theological Soundings

ISRAEL'S SINFULNESS. Moses makes a bold generalization when he says, "You have been rebellious against the LORD from the day that I knew you" (9:24). His primary example is the sin involving the golden calf at Sinai—a flagrant defiance of the prohibition against images in Exodus 20:4–6. But he also says that the same kind of rebellion characterized the whole time in the wilderness (Deut. 9:22–23), a claim well supported by the book of Numbers. For this reason, Israel deserves to be called "stubborn" (used 3x in this section: Deut. 9:6, 13, 27), for stubborn people refuse to change their ways even after repeated correction. Israel may be circumcised in their flesh, but their hearts are uncircumcised—that is, unredeemed (10:16). The inability of Israel to repent raises the question of whether they will ever keep God's law, a question to which we will return. But for now, notice that the condition of Israel is the condition of all humanity. Our sin is not a shallow cut but a terminal cancer. Indeed, so advanced is sin's corrupting power that apart from Christ we are *dead* in our trespasses and the uncircumcision of our sinful nature (Col. 2:13).

ELECTION. God chose Israel apart from any worthiness in themselves. He delights to triumph through a small, sinful people that did not even exist as an independent country before he delivered them (Deut. 4:34; 7:7; 9:24; compare 1 Cor. 1:27–29). And yet, we wonder at the mystery of why God would choose to bless *some* unworthy people and not others. In response to this question, all that God offers is the cryptic phrase that he "set his heart in love on your fathers" (Deut. 10:15; compare 7:7). He does not reveal to us the reasons for his electing love, although it does encourage us that he loves us so graciously (29:29). But we must never confuse election with favoritism. God is not partial (10:17), and he holds Israel to the same standards of holiness as he does the rest of the nations (11:16–17; see "God's Holy People" in Week 7, "Theological Soundings"). Election is a very difficult teaching in Scripture, and in studying it we are ultimately flung back on God's character. If God chooses some and not others, we must trust that this is somehow an expression of his goodness and justice, and in the end we will praise him for it (Rom. 9:21–24). And that, ultimately, is the purpose for the Bible's teaching on election: to replace empty boasts about ourselves (e.g., Deut. 9:4) with boasting about the richness of God's mercy in Christ (Jer. 9:24; Eph. 1:3–6).

Personal Implications

Take some time to reflect on what you have learned from your study of Deuteronomy 9:1–11:32 and how it might apply to your own life today. Make notes below on the personal implications for your walk with the Lord of the (1) *Gospel Glimpses*, (2) *Whole-Bible Connections*, (3) *Theological Soundings*, and (4) this passage as a whole.

1. Gospel Glimpses

2. Whole-Bible Connections

3. Theological Soundings

4. Deuteronomy 9:1–11:32

As You Finish This Unit . . .

Take a moment now to ask for the Lord's blessing and help as you continue in this study of Deuteronomy. Then look back through this unit to reflect on key things the Lord may be teaching you.

Definition

[1] **Gentile** – A non-Jew.

WEEK 7: NOT LIKE THE NATIONS

Deuteronomy 12:1–16:17

▲

With his passionate appeal for Israel to give all of their loyalty to God still ringing in the people's ears (chs. 4–11), Moses now gets specific. The next 15 chapters of the book (Deuteronomy 12–26) expand on the Ten Commandments set out in 5:6–21, which themselves are extensions of the great command to love God with all that they are (6:5). Here God shows us in detail what it means for Israel to love him in the Land of Promise. And as Moses reminds them (and us) at the beginning and end of this section (12:1; 26:16), these laws are from God and thus bear his divine authority.

Amid all of the details of these laws, Moses is anxious that those he instructs should never lose sight of God's grace. Just as the Ten Commandments are the outflow of Israel's identity as the Lord's redeemed people (5:6), so Moses reminds the people repeatedly that they are bound to keep these laws because of God's saving work on their behalf (e.g., 13:5; 15:15; 16:12).

The Big Picture

In contrast to the abominable practices of the nations, God commands Israel to be holy, rejoicing in the Lord alone as the source of all blessing.

49

▶ Reflection and Discussion

Read through the complete passage for this study, Deuteronomy 12:1–16:17. Then review the following questions and record your responses. (For further background, see the *ESV Study Bible*, pages 349–356, or visit esv.org.)

1. The Place for God's Name (12:1–14)

Israel is to destroy the nations' places of worship and set up a new site in a place the Lord will designate. In contrast to the *many* places of the nations, this new site will be a *single* place of the Lord's choosing. List all of the things Israel is to do in this place. What clues does this passage give us about why this place will be so special?

2. Craving Meat (12:15–28)

While some animal offerings were completely burned in sacrifice to the Lord (e.g., the whole burnt offerings described in Leviticus 1), the Israelites were permitted to eat other offerings (e.g., peace offerings; see Lev. 7:15). A peace offering was one of the rare occasions on which meat was consumed in that culture. With the strong insistence in Deuteronomy 12 that Israel is to offer sacrifices only at the place the Lord has chosen, Israel might think that they were not to eat meat anywhere else. This section clarifies that it is perfectly acceptable to eat meat anywhere, as long as it is not offered in a sacrifice. What rules must Israel observe as they eat this "regular" meat?

3. The Seduction of Idolatry (12:29–13:18)

Sin's power is its appeal to our desires (Gen. 3:6). It seduces us, arouses our curiosity, and tempts us with little enticements. In what ways does Moses predict that Israel will be enticed to abandon the Lord (see especially Deut. 12:30; 13:2, 6)?

The punishment for those who lead Israel astray is severe: death by stoning for individuals (13:5, 8–10) and complete destruction for a city (13:15–16). The description of such a city as a "heap forever," not to be "built again" (v. 16), reminds us of Joshua's later sentence on Jericho, which was not to be rebuilt (Josh. 6:26). But in Deuteronomy 13 this fate of destruction is threatened for *Israelite* cities. In other words, leading Israelites to worship other gods makes them Canaanites and therefore puts them under the Canaanites' sentence of total destruction (see Deut. 7:1–5, 16; see also "The Just Destruction of God's Enemies," in Week 5, "Theological Soundings"). What reasons does this passage give for why God is so serious about those who lead others astray?

4. Holiness in Mourning and Eating (14:1–21)

While this section goes into great detail about the kinds of creatures that are acceptable to eat, the main point is not so much about eating as it is about holiness: Israel must not conform to the Canaanite culture of death all around them. They must not eat animals that feast on corpses (e.g., vultures and other scavenger birds; vv. 12–18), nor may they use an agency of life (a goat mother's milk) to cook the baby goat it was intended to sustain (v. 21). In what other ways does Moses warn Israel against associating with the unholiness of death in this passage?

_____

_____

_____

_____

_____

5. The Joy of Tithing (14:22–29)

Israel was to give their tithe to the Levites and the landless (the sojourner, fatherless, and widow) every three years (vv. 28–29). But for the first and second years of this three-year cycle, who gets to enjoy the tithe? Notice the commands to "eat" and "rejoice" in verse 26.

_____

_____

_____

_____

_____

6. As We Forgive Our Debtors (15:1–18)

The Lord redeemed Israel out of slavery once; he will not allow Israel to lapse into slavery again. Israelites must remember who their fellow Israelites are: they are "brothers" (used 7x here), fellow partakers of God's rescue from Egypt, unlike the foreigner (v. 3). What measures does God prescribe here to prevent his people from falling again into slavery?

_____

_____

_____

_____

_____

A close reader may detect an apparent contradiction here: Moses says that "there will be no poor among you" (v. 4) but then says, "there will never cease to be poor in the land" (v. 11; compare Matt. 26:11). (A similar tension appears in Deuteronomy 7 and 12: they are to completely destroy the Canaanites [7:2], yet they are warned against intermarrying with them and imitating their ways

[7:3; 12:30].) What does verse 4 promise if Israel obeys, and what does verse 11 indicate about how likely it is that Israel *will* obey?

_____

_____

_____

_____

7. The Three Feasts (16:1–17)

These three annual feasts (Passover, Weeks, Booths) are described in greater detail in Exodus, Leviticus, and Numbers (see *ESV Study Bible*, p. 355, note on 16:1–17). But Deuteronomy has its own special emphases. What are some of the themes repeated throughout all three feasts? Note repeated words, phrases, and Moses' summary in verses 16–17.

_____

_____

_____

_____

Read through the following three sections on *Gospel Glimpses*, *Whole-Bible Connections*, and *Theological Soundings*. Then take time to consider the *Personal Implications* these sections may have for you.

> ## Gospel Glimpses

THE JOY OF OBEYING GOD. Israel must obey God strictly, with no exceptions. And yet, we completely misread Deuteronomy if we picture God as a tyrannical dictator like Pharaoh. His laws are aimed at bringing about Israel's good (note the repeated phrase "that it may go well with you" and similar language in 4:40; 5:16, 29, 33; 6:3, 18, 24; 10:13; 12:25, 28; 30:16). When Israel obeys God even at great cost (e.g., giving their tithe to the landless; see 14:29), God promises that they will not regret it, for he will crown their obedience with life and blessing (12:28; 13:17; 14:29). This is true liberty, the liberty Christ purchased for us in the gospel: not to be our own masters but to be joyous servants of the King who seeks our good, whose yoke is easy and whose burden is light (Matt. 11:30; John 8:36; Rom. 6:18, 22).

GOD THE GIVER. Again and again God emphasizes that Israel must bring its sacrifices and tithes to the one place he chooses (12:1–14, 17–18, 26–27; 14:22–29). The three great national feasts all happen in this one central place (16:1–17). And yet, once they arrive, God has a surprising command: rejoice (12:7, 12, 18; 14:26; 16:11, 14)! Deuteronomy 14:23–26 even pictures a big party with all the tithe they have brought—all Israel is rejoicing in the lavish gift of the land! But the whole command is crucial: they are to rejoice "*before him.*" What makes the central place unique is that God's presence dwells there (first in the tabernacle,[1] then in the temple) in a special way. Even as God knows that Israel will become wealthy in the land, he is jealous that they never forget that he is the gracious giver of all that they enjoy, lest they lapse into thinking, "My power and the might of my hand have gotten me this wealth" (8:17). The greatest joy comes not in miserly hoarding but in enjoying God's gifts with hearty thankfulness to him and with generous giving to others (1 Tim. 6:17–19; see also 1 Cor. 4:7; James 1:17).

Whole-Bible Connections

THE PLACE FOR THE NAME. The central place of worship will be the "place that the LORD your God will choose out of all your tribes to put his name and make his habitation there" (Deut. 12:5). In contrast to the nations and their gods, whose names will be erased from the land (12:3), God's name will dwell at a particular place in the land like a permanent stone inscription. But better than something etched in stone, the central place will be where God's glory and kingly presence shine forth as nowhere else. Because of the uniqueness of this place as God's dwelling, Israel must go *only there* to worship. Indeed, God even makes provision for their grain and animal offerings to be changed for money if the journey is too far (14:25)! As the story of Israel unfolds, God's name is established in several places where the tabernacle abides (including Shiloh; Jer. 7:12), but his name finally comes to rest in the temple Solomon builds in Jerusalem (2 Sam. 7:13; 1 Kings 8:20; Ps. 76:2). However, the rest of 1–2 Kings records the Israelites' repeated abandonment of the temple by worshiping wherever they please, on every high hill and under every green tree (1 Kings 14:23; 2 Kings 21:3). Eventually God abandons his house in Jerusalem because of the nation's sin (Jer. 12:7; Ezek. 10:18). However, in the new covenant God's glory comes to dwell in his Spirit-filled house, the church (Eph. 2:22; 2 Cor. 6:16; 1 Pet. 2:5), and so now we worship him not in Jerusalem or any other special location but in Spirit and in truth (John 4:20–24).

NO HIGHER LOYALTY. The Lord commands Israel to bring even close family members to justice when they urge abandoning the Lord for other gods (Deut. 13:6–11). The faithful Israelite must cast the first stone even against his loved ones once they are condemned (v. 9). This difficult command reminds us of Abraham, who obeyed God even when commanded to sacrifice Isaac, his beloved son (Gen. 22:1–19). God will brook no rivals in our hearts. We must love him with *all* that we are (Deut. 6:5), and when we must choose between God and beloved family, it is a test of whom we actually love the most (13:3). Jesus calls us to nothing less in the new covenant when he says, "If anyone comes to me and does not hate his own father and mother and wife and children and brothers and sisters, yes, and even his own life, he cannot be my disciple" (Luke 14:26).

Theological Soundings

GOD'S HOLY PEOPLE. The very first command in this section is to avoid worshiping the Lord as the nations worship their gods, and to destroy their places of worship (12:2–4; see 12:30). There is not the slightest hint of compromise here, as though it were acceptable for Israel to incorporate some elements of Canaanite worship into their worship of the Lord. Likewise, chapter 13 deplores the very suggestion that Israel would go after the gods of the nations, and chapter 14 insists that they must not mourn or eat in the ways the nations do, for they are a "people holy to the LORD your God" (14:2, 21; see 7:6; 26:19). To be holy is to be different, set apart in our morality from the rest of the world. God is the standard for how we are to be different: "Be holy, for I am holy" (Lev. 11:44). The New Testament reiterates the command to be holy as God is holy (1 Pet. 1:15–16), but we must remember that the way we show the holy character of our God in the new covenant sometimes differs from how Israel showed their holiness. We now may eat the foods once prohibited to Israel (Acts 10:13–15), but we still eat as holy children, refusing, for example, to participate in the pervasive sins of indulgence and gluttony (Phil. 3:19).

Personal Implications

Take some time to reflect on what you have learned from your study of Deuteronomy 12:1–16:17 and how it might apply to your own life today. Make notes below on the personal implications for your walk with the Lord of the (1) *Gospel Glimpses*, (2) *Whole-Bible Connections*, (3) *Theological Soundings*, and (4) this passage as a whole.

1. Gospel Glimpses

2. Whole-Bible Connections

3. Theological Soundings

4. Deuteronomy 12:1–16:17

As You Finish This Unit . . .

Take a moment now to ask for the Lord's blessing and help as you continue in this study of Deuteronomy. Then look back through this unit to reflect on key things the Lord may be teaching you.

Definition

[1] **Tabernacle** – The tent God commanded Israel to construct at Mount Sinai, in which God dwelt with Israel.

WEEK 8: TRUE JUSTICE AND RIGHTEOUSNESS

Deuteronomy 16:18–21:9

▲

Moses continues his detailed explanation of what it means to keep the Ten Commandments in all of life, a topic that occupies him throughout chapters 12–26 of Deuteronomy. His core emphasis remains the same: Israel must be holy, set apart from the nations. But whereas 12:1–16:17 was primarily about holiness in worship, now he shows how Israel must be different in their government, explaining the godly ideals for four different kinds of leaders: (1) judges, (2) priests, (3) the king, and (4) prophets (16:18–18:22). We also hear about cities of refuge (a protection for those who kill a person accidentally), laws for warfare, and the process for atoning for unsolved murders (19:1–21:9).

The rallying cry for this portion of Deuteronomy is "Justice, and only justice, you shall follow, that you may live and inherit the land that the LORD your God is giving you" (16:20). The land may be a paradise of good food and wealth, but the people are still tainted by sin, and Deuteronomy shows how God has appointed leaders to restrain wickedness through just consequences.

The Big Picture

The Lord entrusts Israel's rulers with the crucial task of implementing justice and righteousness in the land.

> ## Reflection and Discussion

Read through the complete passage for this study, Deuteronomy 16:18–21:9. Then review the following questions and record your responses. (For further background, see the *ESV Study Bible*, pages 356–361, or visit esv.org.)

1. Just Judges (16:18–20)

The appointment of judges to settle legal matters recalls the origins of this institution in Deuteronomy 1:9–18. There Moses exhorted the judges to bear in mind that any distortion of justice is completely intolerable, because "the judgment is God's" (1:17). That is, when the judges hand down a judgment, they express God's own authority (see 17:9–12!) and represent him to the people. In Deuteronomy 16:18–20, what practices does Moses warn about that would subvert justice?

2. Due Process (17:2–13; 19:15–21)

Legal cases can appear clear-cut when they are not, and many may believe a case will lead to certain conviction when the accused is actually innocent. Due process protects the accused from drummed-up charges and false witnesses and gives a chance for truth to prevail (Prov. 18:17; compare 1 Kings 21:1–14). What safeguards do these two texts prescribe to protect Israelites from injustice?

3. The King after God's Heart (17:14–20)

As with the other offices, Moses' intention in addressing kings here is not to give a full description of the king's responsibilities. Instead, he focuses on matters of temptation. What temptations will the king face, and what antidote does Moses offer for these temptations? (Note the way "for himself" is used in vv. 16–17 [3x], but then comes the surprising use of the same phrase in v. 18.)

4. Provision for the Levites (18:1–8)

The Levites have special roles in Israel, including care for the tabernacle (10:8), stewardship of God's Word (17:18; 31:25–26), and rendering of judgment (17:9; 21:5). But even though the Levites do not work the ground, Deuteronomy repeatedly insists (especially in this passage) that the Levites have a right to receive the produce of the land like the rest of Israel (see also 12:12; 14:29). Why, according to this passage, is God so concerned that the Levites receive the produce of the ground? (See also Neh. 13:10.)

5. Knowing Rightly (18:9–22)

The occult practices listed in verses 10–11 are not always a sham but may tap into spiritual forces that are very real, and also very dangerous (see 13:1–3; 1 Sam. 28:8–19). According to this passage, what good and holy source of revelation has God appointed for Israel, and how does God enable his people to recognize what is truly from him?

WEEK 8: TRUE JUSTICE AND RIGHTEOUSNESS

6. The Cities of Refuge (19:1–13)

Moses set apart cities of refuge on the east of the Jordan in Deuteronomy 4:41–43. Now he states that three more must be selected west of the Jordan once they have entered the land, and he clarifies the purpose of these cities. How do these cities serve the cause of justice, and who is entitled to their protection? (For more background, see Num. 35:9–34.)

7. Warfare, Far and Near (20:1–20)

This chapter divides into three sections. The first and third sections (vv. 1–9 and vv. 19–20) prescribe laws for warfare in all contexts, while the second section distinguishes between war against peoples far away (vv. 10–15) and war against peoples close by (vv. 16–18). While the destruction that the Lord authorizes in this passage may alarm us (see "The Just Destruction of God's Enemies" in Week 5, "Theological Soundings"), the purpose here is to curb sin and injustice. How do these laws curb sin and injustice?

8. Unsolved Murder (21:1–9)

Wicked deeds done in secret do not escape the Lord's notice. Innocent blood cries out to him and threatens to bring his judgment upon Israel (Gen. 4:10; 1 Kings 21:19; Jer. 2:34). When no murderer can be found for a slain person, who bears the responsibility of atoning for the crime, and how do they accomplish this atonement?

Read through the following three sections on *Gospel Glimpses, Whole-Bible Connections*, and *Theological Soundings*. Then take time to consider the *Personal Implications* these sections may have for you.

▶ Gospel Glimpses

JESUS THE TRUE PROPHET. In the face of all counterfeit forms of spiritual insight, which lead only to death (Gen. 3:1, 4–5; Deut. 13:1–11; 18:9–14, 20), the Lord stands as the true God who makes himself known (Deut. 4:1–8; 30:11–14). Moses is God's great instrument of revelation, declaring all that God has commanded him (Deut. 1:3). But in Deuteronomy 18:15–19 we see how the Lord will continue to speak to Israel after Moses' death: he will raise up "a prophet like Moses" who will speak on God's behalf. On the one hand, this passage points to all true prophets who come after Moses, who speak not of their own accord but say only what God appoints them to say (Deut. 18:18; Jer. 20:9; 2 Pet. 1:21; compare Jer. 23:16, 21). But these prophets (Moses included) minister the old covenant, which convicts Israel of their sin but lacks the power to overcome sin's tyranny (Jer. 31:31–34; Rom. 3:20), and therefore Paul calls their ministry a "ministry of death" (2 Cor. 3:7). For this reason, Moses and the prophets point beyond themselves to Christ, *the* prophet specifically spoken of in Deuteronomy 18:18 (John 5:46; 1 Pet. 1:10–12). Christ is the climactic revelation of God and is himself God (John 14:6, 9), mediating a new and better covenant (Heb. 8:6; 12:24). Indeed, when Christ appears on the Mount of Transfiguration with Moses and Elijah—the two great prophets of the old covenant—God the Father identifies Christ as *the* prophet who was to come, who is more than a servant, being God's own Son (Heb. 1:1–2; 3:5–6; compare Jer. 7:25). And God urges us, in the words of Deuteronomy 18:15: "Listen to him" (Luke 9:35).

JESUS THE TRUE JUDGE, PRIEST, AND KING. Jesus not only embodies all that God envisioned the prophets to be; he also is the ideal of the other three offices in this section: the true judge, priest, and king. As the great judge, he will dispense true, impartial judgment on the last day (Acts 17:31; Rom. 2:16). As the great priest, he offered the one true atoning sacrifice, in addition to fulfilling all of the responsibilities of the Levites (Heb. 10:10). And as the great king, he does not devote himself to the lusts of the flesh but treasures the law in his heart. In all of these offices we find templates for the multifaceted work of our Savior. But we can say more. Christ not only fulfills these roles; he surpasses them (we could say he "hyper-fulfills" them!). His sacrifice and judgment are so perfect and final that he need not perform these tasks again. As king he will not merely "continue long in his kingdom" (Deut. 17:20); he will reign forever!

61

Whole-Bible Connections

FAILED KINGSHIP. The kings of Israel will face terrible temptation to use their authority for themselves, selfishly hoarding military power, money, and wives (Deut. 17:14–17). If they succumb, they will become just like the kings of the nations—exploiters rather than servants (1 Sam. 8:10–18). It then sends a chill down our spines to read how Solomon, for all his wisdom, fails on all three fronts! He accumulates so much gold that silver is not considered valuable in his days (1 Kings 10:14, 21); he amasses thousands of horses and chariots, even importing them from Egypt (1 Kings 10:26, 28; strictly forbidden in Deut. 17:16!); and he takes 700 wives and 300 concubines (1 Kings 11:3). These wives were not only for sexual gratification but were also for political alliances (1 Kings 3:1), thus showing that his trust was in military arms, not in the Lord. It is not surprising, then, to read of Solomon's apostasy later in life, for all these counterfeit gods—and especially his wives—led him astray (1 Kings 11:3–4). Let us therefore seek not to be deluded into making empty idols our hope, for the Lord alone is the wellspring of life.

Theological Soundings

BALANCED JUSTICE. A key concern of justice is balanced redress for wrongs incurred: "Life for life, eye for eye, tooth for tooth, hand for hand, foot for foot" (Deut. 19:21). Far from a barbaric principle of reparation that leads to unending violence (one side striking another, the other striking back, and on and on), this principle urges restraint: no one will suffer more punishment than they deserve. Moreover, since the punishment is inflicted by the state, not by individuals, the possibility of one brother striking another, followed by the other striking back, is avoided. With the punishment imposed by God-given authorities, the matter is resolved.

PURGING THE EVIL FROM ISRAEL. What about when the crime is so severe that the just reparation is death? When someone takes a life, his own life is required (Gen. 9:6). Likewise, when someone blasphemes against God himself and leads others astray to their spiritual death, the punishment is death (Deut. 13:8–9). In these situations, Deuteronomy repeatedly says that Israel must "purge the evil from your midst" (Deut. 13:5; 17:7, 12; 19:19; 22:21, 22, 24; 24:7). Failure to do so jeopardizes the whole nation, who will then corporately bear the guilt for their failure to judge justly (21:8). Paul echoes the same imperative in the new covenant when he quotes Deuteronomy, saying that the church must "Purge the evil person from among you" (1 Cor. 5:13). In the new covenant, however, we purge the evil from among us not by stoning (since the church is not a civil government, as Israel was) but by the patient application of church discipline (1 Cor. 5:9–13; see especially v. 13), and in God's grace this new covenant purging may even lead to the sinner's restoration prior to the great day of God's justice (1 Cor. 5:5; Rev. 21:8).

Personal Implications

Take some time to reflect on what you have learned from your study of Deuteronomy 16:18–21:9 and how it might apply to your own life today. Make notes below on the personal implications for your walk with the Lord of the (1) *Gospel Glimpses*, (2) *Whole-Bible Connections*, (3) *Theological Soundings*, and (4) this passage as a whole.

1. Gospel Glimpses

2. Whole-Bible Connections

3. Theological Soundings

4. Deuteronomy 16:18–21:9

As You Finish This Unit . . .

Take a moment now to ask for the Lord's blessing and help as you continue in this study of Deuteronomy. Then look back through this unit to reflect on key things the Lord may be teaching you.

WEEK 9: ALL OF LIFE

Deuteronomy 21:10–25:19

▲

We now come to the last series of laws, which show how the great command to love the Lord applies to the smallest details of life. The legislation here focuses on the fifth through the tenth commandments, dealing with parents and children, husbands and wives, theft, false testimony, and greed. Moses' purpose is not to be exhaustive, as though these laws covered every possible situation. Instead, he illustrates how the Ten Commandments apply in specific cases so that we can truly understand the heart of these commands. When we do so, we begin to see the breadth of God's law: the command not to steal means that an Israelite must not have different weights for cheating his brother out of a fair trade (Deut. 25:13). It also means that a worker must be paid for his work without delay (24:15). In the same way, Jesus challenges us that not murdering or committing adultery includes what we think in our hearts (Matt. 5:21–30). Indeed, God's law governs *all* of life.

The Big Picture

Moses illustrates how loving God and neighbor applies to specific situations so that we might learn to apply God's commands justly and faithfully.

▶ Reflection and Discussion

Read through the complete passage for this study, Deuteronomy 21:10–25:19. Then review the following questions and record your responses. (For further background, see the *ESV Study Bible*, pages 361–367, or visit esv.org.)

Note: Because of the large number of small units in this section, we will not step through each unit one-by-one. Instead, we have grouped them by theme.

1. Marriage and Divorce (21:10–14; 22:13–30; 24:1–5)

These laws confront disturbing circumstances: a woman ensnared in war; rape; adultery; divorce. It is vital to understand that God does not condone the circumstances behind these laws (e.g., a man seizing a woman in war [21:10–14]; a man divorcing a woman for some trivial reason [24:1–4]; polygamy [21:15–17]). We know from other texts that such actions are wrong (Matt. 5:31–32; Titus 1:6). Instead of attacking these sins, however, God seeks to show how mercy and justice should prevail even in these deeply broken situations. Given that women had very little opportunity to provide for themselves in ancient Israelite society, how does God protect them with these laws?

2. Integrity (21:15–17; 23:21–23; 25:13–16)

These passages may seem dissimilar, but they all concern the temptation to skirt our duties. How do these laws call us to integrity?

3. Heinous Sins (21:18–21; 24:7)

Both of these laws call for the death penalty for transgressions we may not immediately recognize as being worthy of death. God's purpose is to "purge the evil from your midst." What is so heinous about these sins?

4. Dignity Even in Punishment (21:22–23; 25:1–3)

Even a grievous offender is a person made in God's image, to be treated with respect when he is punished. The ancient world was filled with hideous punishments that left criminals not only mangled in body but also covered with shame. How do these laws restrain the punishment of offenders?

5. Concern for One's Neighbor (22:1–4, 8; 23:19–20; 24:6, 10–15)

Note the repeated word "brother" in these verses. Israel is not allowed to forget that their fellow Israelites are people like them, and God calls them to seek each other's good, just as we would do for our own family members. How do the scenarios in these laws highlight the kinds of occasions when it would be tempting to forget this principle?

6. Creational Order (22:5–7, 9–11)

The laws against mixing (vv. 5, 9–11) seem to express God's concern for creational order: he made animals and vegetation "according to their own kinds" (Gen. 1:12, 21, 24–25), and he distinguished people from each other as male and female (Gen. 1:27). The law concerning a mother bird and her eggs (Deut. 22:6–7) focuses on another aspect of creation, that of stewardship (Gen. 1:26, 28). How does this law reflect how Israel should relate to the land and its creatures (see Deut. 20:19–20; 25:4)?

7. Caring for Those on the Fringe (23:15–16, 24–25; 24:17–22)

Deuteronomy constantly challenges the tendency of the rich to hoard their wealth (see Luke 12:15–21). Who are the people these laws protect, and how does God provide for them?

8. Offspring (25:5–12)

In the old covenant, property in the Promised Land was passed down from father to son. Sons would also bear their father's name by genealogy (e.g., Ezra 7:1–5). In this way, when we view the children as one with their fathers, and fathers living on through their children, we see an Old Testament shadow of the everlasting life offered through Christ. How does this background illumine the concerns in these laws?

Read through the following three sections on *Gospel Glimpses*, *Whole-Bible Connections*, and *Theological Soundings*. Then take time to consider the *Personal Implications* these sections may have for you.

Gospel Glimpses

ACT REDEEMED. We do not obey so that we will be saved. We obey because we *are* saved and are now living out our new identity in Christ (Rom. 6:1–2; Eph. 2:8–10). The same principle is at work in Deuteronomy. We already saw that the statement of how God saved Israel from bondage in Egypt *precedes* the call to obey the Ten Commandments (Deut. 5:6–21). As we have gone through these laws in Deuteronomy, we have seen Moses frequently drawing our attention to how the exact commands God gives to the people express who they are as redeemed former slaves (e.g., 13:5, 10; 14:1–2; 15:15; 16:1, 3, 12; 17:16; 24:17–18). In this section, 24:19–22 is a poignant example. Israel must not harvest every last grape, olive, or wheat sheaf from their fields, but rather they are to leave the gleanings for the sojourner, the fatherless, and the widow. These three landless groups would then have an opportunity to gather food to live on (see Ruth 2:16). The gospel principle is this: You are no longer slaves, so do not turn the Promised Land into a new Egypt by reducing these underprivileged groups to slavery because of their hunger. You who have received grace, show grace to others!

DIVORCE AND A NEW BEGINNING. Some of these laws point us to Christ in surprising ways. Deuteronomy 24:1–4 considers the case of a divorced woman who afterward is joined to another man. This woman is forbidden to return to her first husband, for doing so would trivialize the marriage bond and thus would be an "abomination before the LORD" (v. 4). This law reemerges in a grand scale in God's relationship with Israel. God, the groom, married Israel, the bride, at Sinai (Jer. 2:2). But Israel committed spiritual adultery by worshiping other gods (Jer. 2:20, 32), and God responded justly by "divorcing" his people, sending them away into exile (Jer. 3:8; recall that adultery is the only legitimate cause for divorce apart from abandonment by an unbeliever: Matt. 5:32; 1 Cor. 7:15). In this case, Jeremiah asks, how can Israel ever be joined to God again, if God is to be faithful to his own law (Jer. 3:1)? The answer is given in the death of Christ. In Christ's crucifixion, both bride and groom died, and in his resurrection both were made new (Rom. 7:1–4). In this way, the old has passed away, and God's people are raised anew as a spotless virgin, in order that "You may belong to another, to him who has been raised from the dead" (Rom. 7:4).

Whole-Bible Connections

RIGHT WORSHIP. The laws in Deuteronomy 23:1–6 (concerning people forbidden to enter the assembly of the Lord in worship) may seem unjustly discriminatory to outsiders, the disabled, and others, but there is a deeper rationale at work here. As Leviticus makes clear, only those who are free from disease, physical flaws, and contact with death may be considered "clean" and therefore fit for worship (Lev. 13:3; 21:11, 17–23; see Deut. 24:8–9). In the Old Testament, God's tabernacle is a picture of the new creation he is inaugurating on earth. He allows only the whole to approach, showing how he will heal and restore our bodies in the resurrection (1 Cor. 15:42–44; Rev. 21:4). By forbidding all signs of the brokenness of the old creation (see Gen. 3:16–19) in the tabernacle, God is showing us how perfect the new creation will be. Even now, in the new covenant, all believers—Gentiles, lepers, the disabled—are reckoned as *already* made new in Christ and are welcomed into his presence (Eph. 2:5–6; 2 Cor. 5:17).

NOT MUZZLING THE OX. Deuteronomy 25:4, which forbids muzzling an ox while it treads out the grain, is referenced twice in the New Testament by Paul (1 Cor. 9:9; 1 Tim. 5:18). The oxen would crush grain that had been harvested so that the nourishing seed kernels could be separated from the husks. To muzzle an ox would keep it from eating some of the seed, yielding more seed at the end. By barring the muzzling of an ox, the Lord is showing us that even oxen should enjoy some of the fruit of their labors, and further, he is encouraging kindness to animals (see Prov. 12:10). But when Paul applies this text, he speaks not of agriculture but of financial provision for pastors. This use of Deuteronomy in the New Testament gives us a pattern to follow when applying Old Testament laws to ourselves: we must penetrate to the core moral principle of the law (the "general equity" of it) and then consider how this law should shape our lives in a new covenant context.

Theological Soundings

THE WEIGHTIER MATTERS OF THE LAW. This section repeatedly illustrates what Jesus referred to when he said we must not obey only the strict details of what God requires but also "the weightier matters of the law: justice and mercy and faithfulness" (Matt. 23:23). In other words, there are times when love dictates that we must let go of certain tight readings of the law. A man may own an entire field and be entitled to *all* its produce, but love dictates that he leave the gleanings for the poor (Deut. 24:19–22). A criminal's punishment may call for more than 40 lashes according to strict justice, but regard for his humanity dictates that no more than 40 be given (25:3). A creditor may deserve to keep a poor man's cloak overnight as a pledge for the repayment of his debt, but he should give it back to the debtor all the same so that he has something to sleep in (24:12–13). Only when we truly internalize the value system at the heart of God's law—that is, love of God and love of neighbor (Matt. 22:37–40)—can we rightly apply God's law.

Personal Implications

Take some time to reflect on what you have learned from your study of Deuter- onomy 21:10–25:19 and how it might apply to your own life today. Make notes below on the personal implications for your walk with the Lord of the (1) *Gospel Glimpses*, (2) *Whole-Bible Connections*, (3) *Theological Soundings*, and (4) this pas- sage as a whole.

1. Gospel Glimpses

2. Whole-Bible Connections

3. Theological Soundings

4. Deuteronomy 21:10–25:19

As You Finish This Unit . . .

Take a moment now to ask for the Lord's blessing and help as you continue in this study of Deuteronomy. Then look back through this unit to reflect on key things the Lord may be teaching you.

WEEK 10: THE BLESSING AND THE CURSE

Deuteronomy 26:1–29:1

▲

The laws of Deuteronomy now culminate in a final command to present the firstfruits of the harvest (ch. 26). This command is far from a mere add-on. In offering the produce of the land, Israel remembers each year the core of their identity: they were once not a people, but now they are the people of God.

Having completed the full-orbed picture of Israel's responsibility to love the Lord with all their heart, soul, and might (chs. 4–26), Moses then moves to the consequences of obedience and disobedience (chs. 27–28). Israel is on the cusp of either life or death, and there is no possibility for life if Israel chooses the path of sin. Curses are pronounced against individuals who commit iniquity in secret (27:15–26), and Moses also depicts with gruesome detail the curses that will come against the nation as a whole if they corporately turn from the Lord (28:15–68).

The contrast with the consequences if Israel chooses obedience could not be more extreme. The picture of blessing (28:1–14) is the exact opposite of the curse: Israel will enjoy the intense goodness of the Lord in all of life, to his glory and their joy.

The Big Picture

If the people of Israel remember who they are and act in accordance with the Lord's will, they will enjoy tremendous blessing. If they do not, they will face the horrible curses of the covenant.

Reflection and Discussion

Read through the complete passage for this study, Deuteronomy 26:1–29:1. Then review the following questions and record your responses. (For further background, see the *ESV Study Bible*, pages 367–372, or visit esv.org.)

1. Firstfruits and Faith (26:1–15)

The head of each Israelite household must bring the firstfruits from the land each year (probably during the Feast of Weeks; see 16:9–12). At this time he is to reaffirm his faith with a simple creed (26:5–11), much as Christians do when we recite the Nicene Creed (or a similar creed) together. According to verses 5–11, what are the key things Israel must remember and confess?

In 26:12–15 the focus shifts from the beginning of the harvest to the end, when the tithe is paid. Every third year, when the tithe is given to the landless in their town instead of being brought to the central sanctuary (see 14:28–29), Israel will come before the Lord without their produce in hand. At this time, they will make a statement of innocence, declaring that they really have given it to the needy and have not kept it for themselves. Look back at 14:28–29 and other texts that describe the blessing that comes when Israel is not tightfisted (15:10, 12–18; 23:20; 24:19; see also Mal. 3:10). How do these pictures of blessing help Israel to have the faith they need to keep this command?

2. Covenant Ratification (26:16–19)

A covenant is formally put in place when the two parties say "I do," much like when a bride and groom make their vows at a wedding. Israel did this at Sinai when God gave them the law, declaring them to be his people, and they responded by saying, "All the words that the LORD has spoken we will do" (Ex. 24:3). Now Moses records that the people of Israel have renewed their vows on the plains of Moab (the geographic setting for the book of Deuteronomy). What does each party (God and Israel) declare to the other in this act of covenant renewal (vv. 17–19)?

3. Curses for Secret Sins (27:1–26)

Moses now looks ahead to when Israel enters the land, ordering a special ceremony to take place in the Promised Land at Shechem, flanked by Mount Ebal to the north and Mount Gerizim to the south (a ceremony that Joshua carries out; see Josh. 8:30–35). How does the arrangement described in verses 1–8 (writing the law on the stones, building an altar, offering sacrifices, eating and rejoicing) set the tone for Israel's life in the land?

The curses pronounced in verses 9–26 address sins that are done in secret and perhaps may never be confronted in human courts of law. How do these solemn curses challenge the lie that there are no consequences for sin if no one ever finds out?

4. The Blessing (28:1–14)

What spheres of life are addressed in this wonderful list of blessings? How do these blessings speak of the good ways God can work in those areas of life?

5. The Curse (28:15–68)

This list of curses is one of the most disturbing passages of Scripture, especially when Moses describes the siege by foreign invaders (vv. 52–57). How do these curses describe, in increasing intensity, a loss of the blessings listed in verses 1–14? What is the last and climactic curse of the covenant (vv. 64–68)?

Read Genesis 17:6–8, which describes the core promises God made to Abraham (see "Placing Deuteronomy in the Larger Story," in Week 1). How do the blessings in Deuteronomy 28 picture the fulfillment of these promises to Abraham, and how do the curses in Deuteronomy 28 picture the removal of what was promised to him?

Read through the following three sections on *Gospel Glimpses, Whole-Bible Connections*, and *Theological Soundings*. Then take time to consider the *Personal Implications* these sections may have for you.

Gospel Glimpses

HE BECAME A CURSE FOR US. Deuteronomy 28:15–68 describes the horrific outpouring of God's wrath that will come upon Israel for their disobedience. Just as the land foreshadows heaven, so do the curses foreshadow hell in all its terror. The astonishing proclamation of the gospel is that *God himself* became a man so that he could endure the curse of the covenant on our behalf. As a sinful people, we—like Israel—are unable to keep God's law, and "Cursed be everyone who does not abide by all things written in the Book of the Law" (Gal. 3:10, quoting Deut. 27:26). But Jesus Christ, being God in the flesh, kept the law perfectly and thus deserved the blessings of the covenant (Rom. 5:18). Instead, he received the covenant curses on the cross (Gal. 3:13; see Deut. 21:23). Why this apparent reversal of justice? Jesus was actually made to *be* sin for us, bearing our iniquities in his body on the cross (2 Cor. 5:21; 1 Pet. 2:24), and therefore he was the just recipient of the Father's wrath. As horrific as the curses in Deuteronomy 28:15–68 are, they are a mere shadow of the ultimate wrath Jesus experienced for us on the cross. What a Savior!

Whole-Bible Connections

A TREASURED POSSESSION. Despite Israel's fickleness and rebellion, in Deuteronomy 26:18–19 God dotes on his holy people as his "treasured possession," set high above the nations "in praise and in fame and in honor." With the resurrection of Christ, these Israel-only titles are transferred to the church, the true Israel and ultimate people of God (1 Pet. 1:7; 2:9–10; Eph. 1:18; compare Isa. 19:25).

THE COVENANT CURSES IN HISTORY. Deuteronomy 28 provides a framework for understanding all of Israel's history, and the rest of the Old Testament constantly alludes to this chapter. When Israel is without water (1 Kings 17:1), we remember Deuteronomy 28:22–24. When Israel is defeated in battle (1 Sam. 4:1–11), we remember Deuteronomy 28:25. When Israel is finally destroyed by a marauding nation and exiled from the land (2 Kings 17:1–23; 25:1–21), we remember Deuteronomy 28:49–68. One of the prophets' central messages is that these terrible events are happening not because God is too weak to prevent them but because he himself is inflicting these calamities because of his just wrath (Jer. 5:19; 21:4–7). Recognizing the Lord's hand behind these calamities should stir Israel to repentance, acknowledging that their own sin has brought these afflictions upon them.

Theological Soundings

GOD'S HOLY ANGER. If God's command to destroy the Canaanites seems horrifying (see "The Just Destruction of God's Enemies" in Week 5, "Theological Soundings"), so also does the detailed list of horrors he will bring upon his own people if they disobey. We wince to read, "The Lord will take delight in bringing ruin upon you and destroying you" (Deut. 28:63). As a perfectly sovereign God, he always does what most pleases him, and we see even in the crucifixion that it "pleased" the Lord to crush his Son (Isa. 53:10 KJV). God is pleased with pouring out these curses not because he is a sadist (see Ezek. 18:23), but because he is *just*. The horror of the punishment fits the horror of the crime: Israel sacrifices their children to false gods in the fire, so they will be left few in number. Israel exploits the land, so they will be removed from the land. Israel willfully pursues other gods, so they will serve other gods in a foreign land.

COVENANT BLESSINGS AND CURSES TODAY. Israel was to interpret events in their nation's life in light of the blessings and curses of Deuteronomy 28. Success in battle showed that God was with them (28:7), while defeat showed that he was against them (28:25). The book of Job demonstrates that this principle cannot be applied mechanically, as though every sorrow we undergo is God's retribution for our sin, for Job was blameless (Job 1:1). But the basic principle stands: a person who fears God and who is surrounded by good things is a person whom God has blessed (Ps. 128:4). What about in the new covenant? Now our expectations pivot as we consider our Savior, who was first crucified, then glorified. In this present time, we expect that suffering will mark those who follow Christ (Matt. 10:24–25; John 16:20, 33; 2 Tim. 3:12; 1 Pet. 4:12), and Jesus even calls "blessed" those who suffer for his sake in this present age (Matt. 5:11–12). We are blessed because our sufferings mark us as heirs of genuine blessedness, which will be revealed ultimately in the new creation to come (Phil. 1:21; 3:7–11).

CREEDS. The confession of faith that Israel was to make each year, found in Deuteronomy 26:5–11, shows us the importance of remembering what God has done for us. It also reminds us of our unity with the rest of the people of God. In our creeds, we declare that we are members of the same story, a story governed by the gracious God who loves to save sinners. The Christian church does well to incorporate this vital and joyful practice of collective remembrance in its own ongoing life.

Personal Implications

Take some time to reflect on what you have learned from your study of Deuteronomy 26:1–29:1 and how it might apply to your own life today. Make notes below on the personal implications for your walk with the Lord of the (1) *Gospel Glimpses*, (2) *Whole-Bible Connections*, (3) *Theological Soundings*, and (4) this passage as a whole.

1. Gospel Glimpses

2. Whole-Bible Connections

3. Theological Soundings

4. Deuteronomy 26:1–29:1

As You Finish This Unit . . .

Take a moment now to ask for the Lord's blessing and help as you continue in this study of Deuteronomy. Then look back through this unit to reflect on key things the Lord may be teaching you.

WEEK 11: THE FUTURE OF ISRAEL

Deuteronomy 29:2–31:29

▲

The Place of the Passage

Having preached at length on the Lord's great vision for his relationship with Israel, Moses brings his sermon to its climax. If obedience alone is the path of life; if death is the only alternative; if all Israel's future hangs in the balance—then choose life (30:15–20)! It is not as though God has been unclear on what he expects of Israel (30:11–14) or on what will happen to them if they disobey (29:16–28), nor has he been unfaithful to them in the past (29:2–9). Nothing stands in the way of Israel's taking the path of life.

Nothing, that is, except Israel itself. Despite his impassioned plea to choose life, Moses is certain that Israel will choose the path of death (31:16, 19–29). So great is the power of sin that Israel could have everything they need for a life of obedience and blessing and still choose sin. This dismal dose of realism would leave us with bleak hopes for Israel's future were it not for the fact that God had already planned a way for his grace to triumph (30:1–10).

The Big Picture

Even though Israel must obey to be blessed, they will not. Nevertheless, God has planned a way for his grace to triumph.

> ### Reflection and Discussion

Read through the complete passage for this study, Deuteronomy 29:2–31:29. Then review the following questions and record your responses. (For further background, see the *ESV Study Bible*, pages 372–376, or visit esv.org.)

1. A Covenant People (29:2–15)

As a culmination of the laws and consequences he has outlined (chs. 4–28), Moses surveys Israel's recent past and describes how Israel is now renewing their covenant with God. Based on these verses, how does Moses define Israel? Who is a member of it? What makes the Israelites who they are? What is special about them?

2. A Temptation and a Warning (29:16–28)

Having the everlasting promises of God and being exalted high above other nations (see 29:13; 26:18–19) leads to unique temptations for Israel. In particular, they could so emphasize God's special favor to themselves as to think they would face no consequences for their sin (29:19; see Jer. 7:8–10). Describe the poignant picture Moses paints here to confront this false thinking.

3. Hope for the Future (30:1–10)

This text is one of the most important passages in the entire Old Testament. In a staggering act of prophecy, Moses by the inspiration of God foretells the entire history of God's people. Because of Israel's incorrigible sinfulness, Moses knows (even before they have entered the land!) that they will certainly fall into sin and be exiled (v. 1). What will take place after they have been exiled? Summarize the timeline given in verses 1–10.

4. The Word Is Very Near You (29:29; 30:11–14)

God does not reveal himself exhaustively (29:29), but neither does he completely hide himself (see 4:7–8). According to these verses, what has God revealed to Israel, and for what purpose?

5. Choose Life (30:15–20)

These verses, especially verses 19–20, are widely regarded as the climax of the entire book of Deuteronomy. What is Moses' great plea to Israel, and how does this plea summarize the book as a whole? Notice especially how he seeks to motivate Israel using the repeated words "life" and "live."

6. Looking to the Future, Far and Near (31:1–29)

Having made his last great plea, Moses now makes concrete preparations for his death. He names as his successor Joshua, whom the Lord has commissioned

(31:1–8, 14–15, 23). What will be Joshua's responsibilities, not just in terms of actions but also in terms of attitude?

Moses also leaves behind a written copy of the law (31:9–13, 24–29) and a special song (31:19–22; 31:30–32:47). What are the Levites supposed to do with the book, and how will both the law and the song function as a "witness" in the days to come?

Read through the following three sections on *Gospel Glimpses, Whole-Bible Connections*, and *Theological Soundings*. Then take time to consider the *Personal Implications* these sections may have for you.

Gospel Glimpses

GRACE IN THE END. Moses had hinted in Deuteronomy 4:29–31 that after God removed Israel from the land in judgment, the nation would somehow return to the Lord. In 30:1–10 Moses expands on this great reversal that will overtake Israel in exile. He promises that when the Israelites return to the Lord with all their heart and soul, the Lord will bring the scattered remnant of his people back to the land and will restore to them blessings even greater than those they enjoyed before. The greatest blessing of all will be the gift of a circumcised heart (30:6), such that Israel will finally be able to obey God without compromise. But if Israel will be so intractably disobedient throughout their history, what reason do we have to believe that they would ever return to the Lord with all their heart and soul, as this passage demands? Indeed, when Israel was in exile and remembered this text (Neh. 1:5–11), their subsequent repentance left much to be desired (see the major moral failures recorded in Neh. 13:4–29). For this reason, Israel remained in a situation of exile (broadly defined as being under the wrath of God; compare Neh. 13:18) even when they were physically back in the Promised Land in Ezra–Nehemiah. This exile came to an end only when the true Israel arrived—Jesus Christ, who loved his Father with all of his heart and soul. By his enduring the baptism of repentance that fulfills all righteousness (Matt. 3:15), and the curse of God on the cross (Gal. 3:13), Jesus opens the way to all the blessings spoken of in Deuteronomy 30:3–10, including the gathering of his people from the far reaches of the earth and the circumcision of their hearts.

Whole-Bible Connections

HEART CIRCUMCISION. Israel is circumcised in the flesh, but not in the heart. This fallen heart condition is what Moses refers to in Deuteronomy 29:4 when he says, "To this day the LORD has not given you a heart to understand or eyes to see or ears to hear." However much Israel may superficially understand what Moses says, the truth of God's Word has not penetrated to their heart of hearts, and so the deception of sin has greater power in their lives. As late as Jeremiah's day (right before the exile in the early 500s BC), Jeremiah is still imploring Israel to circumcise their hearts (Jer. 4:4; compare Deut. 10:16), something they are ultimately incapable of doing. Their hearts remain uncircumcised up through the exile (Lev. 26:41; Jer. 9:26), and even beyond to the time of Christ (Acts 7:51). Only through the work of Christ, who himself was circumcised on our behalf (in his death; see Col. 2:11), can the old power of sin be vanquished. Here at last is the answer not only to Israel's longstanding stubbornness but also to the depravity of all of Adam's race. Now Christ by his Spirit gives us new, circumcised hearts (Rom. 2:28–29). He cuts away our old broken inability to repent and obey and makes us a new creation, freed from bondage to sin and able to obey God from the heart (Rom. 6:17; Gal. 6:15).

Theological Soundings

THE POSSIBILITY OF OBEDIENCE. Deuteronomy 30:11–14, with its emphasis on how doable the law should be, sounds confusing next to Deuteronomy 31:19–29 and its certainty that Israel will fall away from the Lord. Joshua 24:19 even states baldly that Israel is not able to serve the Lord. On the one hand, Deuteronomy 30:11–14 captures the truth that God's law is reasonable. He has made it clear to his people, and its standards are not physically impossible. He has even made provision for their sin by giving them sacrifices so they can renew their relationship with God (see especially the Day of Atonement in Leviticus 16). All of this shows that the law is impossible for Israel because of a shortcoming *not* in the law but in Israel. The entire story of Israel in the Old Testament is a story of apostasy, of affections enslaved to loving what is worthless (Jer. 2:25; 14:10), of hearts that refuse to listen (Jer. 7:25–26), and of wills in stubborn recalcitrance (Jer. 18:11–12). In short, Israel is dead in sin and needs a resurrection! Paul highlights Israel's inability to obey and points us to Christ: "God has done what the law, weakened by the flesh [i.e., our sin nature], could not do" (Rom. 8:3). Being raised up with Christ means we now have new heart-desires, giving us the long-promised power to obey (Jer. 24:7; 31:31–34; Ezek. 36:26–27; Rom. 6:6, 12–18; Eph. 2:5).

THE PURPOSE OF ISRAEL'S HISTORY. Seeing how Israel lacked the power to obey God in the old covenant raises the question of why God ordained such a lengthy period of spiritual weakness. Of course, sometimes we see ways in which God's Spirit breaks into this period of history to give us examples of triumphant faith (Abraham, Joseph, David, Josiah, Daniel, and so on). But these examples do not offset the overall picture of tragic brokenness. While God's ultimate reasons are known only to him (Deut. 29:29), it seems that there is at least one thing we see now with spectacular clarity that we would not have seen without the Old Testament: our tremendous need for *God* to save us.

Personal Implications

Take some time to reflect on what you have learned from your study of Deuteronomy 29:2–31:29 and how it might apply to your own life today. Make notes below on the personal implications for your walk with the Lord of the (1) *Gospel Glimpses*, (2) *Whole-Bible Connections*, (3) *Theological Soundings*, and (4) this passage as a whole.

1. Gospel Glimpses

2. Whole-Bible Connections

3. Theological Soundings

4. Deuteronomy 29:2–31:29

> ### As You Finish This Unit . . .

Take a moment now to ask for the Lord's blessing and help as you continue in this study of Deuteronomy. Then look back through this unit to reflect on key things the Lord may be teaching you.

WEEK 12: CONCLUSION: THE END OF AN ERA

Deuteronomy 31:30–34:12

▲

As we conclude this study of Deuteronomy, we begin by considering the final section of the book, 31:30–34:12. Many of the core themes of the book are reemphasized here, especially in the song found in 32:1–43. We will then review some questions for reflection in light of the entire book of Deuteronomy, with a final identification of Gospel Glimpses, Whole-Bible Connections, and Theological Soundings.

The Place of the Passage

Deuteronomy concludes with three important texts: the great song the Lord taught to Moses (32:1–43), Moses' final words of blessing on Israel (ch. 33), and the account of Moses' death (32:48–52; 34:1–12). The song in chapter 32 summarizes Israel's history in poetic form, even before that history takes place! And as Moses' life draws to a close, we see both the end of the era of his leadership and the beginning of a new era shaped by the writings he has left.

The Big Picture of Deuteronomy 31:30–34:12

Even as Moses departs from the scene of history, his Spirit-inspired words remain to rebuke, direct, and encourage God's people.

Reflection and Discussion

Read through the complete passage for this study, Deuteronomy 31:30–34:12. Then review the following questions and record your responses. (For further background, see the *ESV Study Bible*, pages 376–383, or visit esv.org.)

1. The Song (32:1–43)

The first section of this song (vv. 1–18) speaks of how God will bless Israel by giving them the land (vv. 10–14) but also of how Israel (here called "Jeshurun") will betray God (vv. 15–18). What is it about this betrayal that is such an affront to God? (See also v. 21.)

The next section of the song (vv. 19–35) portrays God's fiery justice upon his people, summoning us to join God in finding his judgment just. But God holds back from destroying Israel completely, for he does not want the unbelieving nations to have the last word (vv. 26–27). In the final section of the song, verses 36–43, we see that *God* has the last word: because of his compassion for Israel (v. 36), he will one day arise to judge his people's enemies. What does God want us to learn about him from this history (see especially vv. 39, 43)?

2. The Blessing (33:1–29)

As with the song in chapter 32, the poetry here is often cryptic, and sometimes we are not certain how "blessed" some of the tribes actually are (e.g., 33:6, 22). Yet the overall tone emphasizes Israel's deep privilege at having the Lord as their God. How does this text give specific expectations of blessedness to certain tribes?

_____

_____

_____

_____

_____

3. The Death of Moses (32:48–52; 34:1–12)

Moses stands as a unique figure in the Old Testament. How do these verses emphasize the special relationship he shared with the Lord?

_____

_____

_____

_____

_____

The Big Picture of Deuteronomy

Deuteronomy stands at a crossroads in Israel's history. Israel is about to go from being a wandering people in the wilderness to being a settled people in the Land of Promise. They are about to transition from the leadership of Moses to that of Joshua. And they are about to face a host of intense temptations to compromise with the nations of the land, especially the temptation to worship other gods.

In the face of these changes, the Lord inspired Moses to preach his final great sermon—the book of Deuteronomy—that not only calls Israel to renewed fidelity but also shows what heartfelt love for the Lord should look like when they enter the land. As a word from the Lord about how Israel is to live in relationship with him, Deuteronomy is not only a sermon but also a covenant document, structured in five parts.

First, Moses surveys the Lord's recent dealings with Israel, reminding them of their failure to enter the land at Kadesh-barnea and of their consequent wandering for 40 years (chs. 1–3). In God's grace, they now have a second opportunity to enter the land, and they must not repeat the sin of the previous generation.

Next, Moses challenges Israel with a call to total loyalty to the Lord (chs. 4–11). Because of the holiness of their God and how he delivered them from Egypt, they must love the Lord with all their heart, soul, and might. Instead of forgetting their past and imitating the nations around them, Israel must remember what God has done and teach their children to obey his commands.

Third, we see in detail what Israel's love for the Lord should look like in the land (chs. 12–26). These chapters sketch key institutions, such as the central sanctuary, the tithe, the three great feasts, and the offices of judge, priest, king, and prophet. Far from providing an exhaustive law code, Moses gives a series of pointed examples illustrating what true faithfulness should look like.

Fourth, Moses reminds the people that their decision to serve the Lord is a matter of life and death (chs. 27–28). Blessing will abound for them if they obey, but curses loom if they disobey. The worst curse is Israel's banishment from the land and from the Lord's presence.

Moses concludes with a sketch of Israel's future (chs. 29–34). Although Israel will certainly fail to keep covenant with God because of their corrupt hearts, God will not fail to keep covenant with them. He will judge them justly, but he will also restore them from exile and grant them a new beginning as his people.

Read through the following three sections on *Gospel Glimpses*, *Whole-Bible Connections*, and *Theological Soundings*. Then take time to consider the *Personal Implications* these sections may have for you.

▶ Gospel Glimpses

From start to finish, Israel's relationship with the Lord is governed by grace. The Lord chose Israel not because of any worthiness in them but because of his unconditional love for them. He redeemed them from Egypt by his great power. And now he is giving them the land as a gift, in keeping with his ancient promises. The laws found in Deuteronomy are themselves grace-laden: the Lord desires his people to rejoice in the land's goodness in his presence, and he requires them to share their wealth with the landless. And even when they fail and are exiled, he will still remember them. Not only do the institutions of Deuteronomy show us Christ (e.g., the prophet like Moses), but so do the terms of Israel's relationship with God: Jesus is the true Israel who secures our blessing through his obedience and who endures the curses of the covenant on our behalf.

Were there any particular passages or themes in Deuteronomy that led you to a fresh understanding and grasp of God's grace to us through Jesus?

Whole-Bible Connections

Applying the book of Deuteronomy to new covenant Christians requires us to remember the contours of redemptive history. Christ fulfills Old Testament shadows in surprising ways, and in comparing our situation to the original audience of Deuteronomy, we must always consider what has remained the same now that Christ has come and what has changed. Whether the old covenant reality in view is the land (showing us the new creation), the central sanctuary (replaced now with the church as the dwelling of God's Spirit), or specific laws and their consequences, Deuteronomy continues to speak to Christians as we reflect on how our unchanging God brings his purposes to their culmination in Christ.

How has this study of Deuteronomy filled out your understanding of the biblical storyline of redemption?

What connections between Deuteronomy and the New Testament were new to you?

> **Theological Soundings**

Deuteronomy confronts us with a God who is not like us. If he is zealous for holiness and terrifying in his judgments, he is also profoundly gracious to Israel. He refuses to give up on them, urging them to find their hope and joy in him alone. Deuteronomy also confronts us with ourselves: the brokenness of our hearts, our tendency to idolatry and empty boasts, and our inability to keep God's law in our own strength.

How has your understanding of the nature and character of God been deepened throughout this study?

What contributions has Deuteronomy made toward your understanding of who Jesus is and what he has accomplished through his life, death, and resurrection?

What, specifically, does Deuteronomy teach us about the human condition and our need of redemption?

Personal Implications

Take some time to reflect on what you have learned from your study of Deuteronomy 31:30–34:12 and how it might apply to your own life today. Make notes below on the personal implications for your walk with the Lord of the (1) *Gospel Glimpses*, (2) *Whole-Bible Connections*, (3) *Theological Soundings*, and (4) this passage as a whole.

1. Gospel Glimpses

2. Whole-Bible Connections

3. Theological Soundings

4. Deuteronomy 31:30–34:12

As You Finish Studying Deuteronomy . . .

We rejoice with you as you finish studying the book of Deuteronomy! May this study become part of your Christian walk of faith, day-by-day and week-by-week throughout all your life. Now we would greatly encourage you to continue to study the Word of God on a week-by-week basis. To continue your study of the Bible, we would encourage you to consider other books in the *Knowing the Bible* series, and to visit www.knowingthebible.org.

Lastly, take a moment again to look back through this study. Review again the notes that you have written, and the things that you have highlighted or underlined. Reflect again on the key themes that the Lord has been teaching you about himself and about his Word. May these things become a treasure for you throughout your life—this we pray in the name of the Father, and the Son, and the Holy Spirit. Amen.